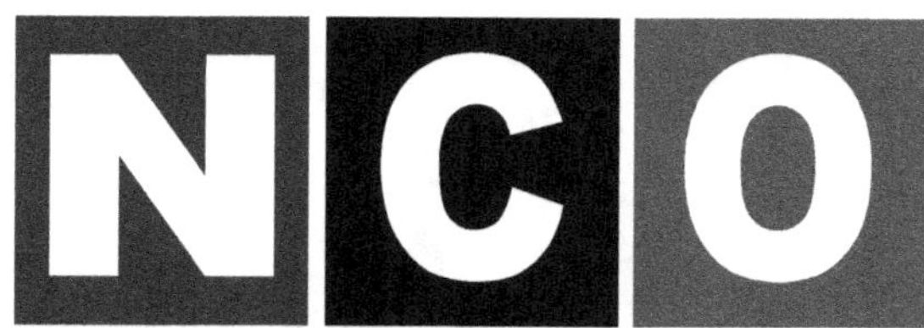

OLYMPIAD WORKBOOK

NATIONAL CYBER OLYMPIAD

01 **Learning Objectives**

02 **Multiple Choice Questions**

03 **HOTS (Achievers Section)**

04 **Model Test Paper**

05 **Answer Keys and Solutions**

06 **OMR Answer Sheet**

V&S PUBLISHERS

Published by:

V&S PUBLISHERS

F-2/16, Ansari road, Daryaganj, New Delhi-110002
☎ 23240026, 23240027 • *Fax:* 011-23240028
✉ info@vspublishers.com • 🌐 www.vspublishers.com

 **Online Brandstore: amazon.in/vspublishers**

Regional Office : Hyderabad
5-1-707/1, Brij Bhawan (Beside Central Bank of India Lane)
Bank Street, Koti, Hyderabad - 500 095
☎ 040-24737290
✉ vspublishershyd@gmail.com

Follow us on:   

BUY OUR BOOKS FROM: | AMAZON | FLIPKART |

© Copyright: **V&S PUBLISHERS**
ISBN 978-81-978176-7-0
New Edition

PUBLISHER'S NOTE

V&S Publishers has carved a significant niche in the publishing industry over the last decade, having successfully published more than 1000 titles across 9 languages spanning over 50 subject categories. Being known for the quality of content, we have built a reputation of excellence and reliability. We have consistently delivered **"Value & Substance"** to our readers, through a wide range of titles across a variety of genres covering school books, fiction and non-fiction that caters to different people from every section of the society.

The **Olympiad Guidebooks for classes 1-10** across all subjects, launched almost a decade ago, under the **GEN X Imprint**, became a go-to-source for the school students in no time, owing to their invaluable and substantive content written in a guidebook pattern,.

Having successfully sold a million copies of the same and in response to demand by both students as well as shopkeepers nationwide; we now present before you our newly launched **Olympiad Workbook Series**, designed for **classes 1-10 across 4 subjects**.

The workbooks are meticulously curated by a team of experienced educators, researchers and subject matter experts, edited by professionals and peer reviewed by teachers. The team has poured its efforts and expertise into creating a crisp and concise workbook which will help and guide the students to the path of success in Olympiad exams. The **MCQs** identified will not only help in scoring top marks in Olympiads but also inculcate a sense of deeper understanding of the subject, by way of solving **HOTS** and referring to complete solutions at the end of the book.

Here we present our new release– **OLYMPIAD WORKBOOK (NCO) CLASS–8** having following features:

- ☞ Based on the latest syllabi
- ☞ MCQs with comprehensive coverage of topics
- ☞ HOTS Questions liberally included
- ☞ A dedicated chapter on logical reasoning
- ☞ Model test paper for thorough practice
- ☞ Sample OMR sheet for real time simulation

We have made sure through our best efforts, that this workbook strictly follows the latest syllabi and patterns of the Olympiad Examination.

As **V&S Publishers** continuously strive to enhance the readability and maintain the credibility of our academic publications, we seek the support of our valuable readers in influencing and enriching the lives of future generations of students.

P.S. While every care has been taken to ensure the correctness of the content, if you come across any error, howsoever minor, do not hesitate to discuss with teachers while pointing that out to us in no uncertain terms.

We wish you all the best for your exams!

DISTINCTIVE FEATURES

01 Learning Objectives

They list the whole chapter as subtopics, helping the teachers to guide children in a step-by-step manner.

02 Multiple Choice Questions

MCQs act as an excellent learning aid, helping you to understand and work on your mistakes.

03 HOTS (Achievers Section)

The High Order Thinking Questions aim to help the student to solve Application-based questions and gain practical understanding of the subject.

04 Model Test Paper

Model test paper are provided at the end of each book, which help the student to test the knowledge which they have gained after thorough reading of all chapters.

05 Answer Key

Detailed Answer Key along with explanations aid the pupil to indentify, understand the mistakes they make during the course of Olympiad preparation.

CONTENTS

FUNDAMENTALS OF COMPUTER-HARDWARE AND SOFTWARE

LEARNING OBJECTIVES

➤ Hardware and its components
➤ Software and Installation

MULTIPLE CHOICE QUESTIONS

1. HDD stands for
   (A) Hard drive disk
   B) Heavy disk drive
   (C) Hard Disk Drive
   (D) Halt disk drive
2. In Microsoft Windows, hardware resources are managed by
   (A) Device supervisor
   (B) Device cleaner
   (C) Device manager
   (D) Manager
3. AVG is
   (A) Movie player
   (B) Antivirus
   (C) Device driver
   (D) Word processor
4. It is an Ethernet card and a network adaptor.
   (A) HDD
   (B) NIC
   (C) AMD
   (D) DVD
5. It is usually the largest data storage device in a computer.
   (A) DVD
   (B) Hard disk
   (C) CD
   (D) Pen drive
6. It is also called the logic board.
   (A) Sound card
   (B) Optical drive
   (C) Motherboard
   (D) Video card
7. The motherboard also has
   (A) Sound card
   (B) DVD
   (C) CD
   (D) Floppy Disk
8. It mediates communication between the CPU and the other components of the system, including the main memory.
   (A) ROM
   (B) RAM
   (C) Sound card
   (D) Chipset

9. Popular manufacturer of the motherboard is
   (A) Seagate
   (A) Western Digital
   (C) Hitachi
   (D) ABIT

10. The CMOS battery is same as the
   (A) Mobile battery
   (B) Car battery
   (C) Watch battery
   (D) Torch battery

11. It is also called the brain of the computer.
   (A) RAM
   (B) ROM
   (C) Power supply
   (D) CPU

12. To dissipate the heat, CPU is connected to the
   (A) Power supply
   (B) Motherboard
   (C) Heat sink and fan
   (D) Sound card

13. It is also called primary memory.
   (A) CD
   (B) DVD
   (C) ROM
   (D) RAM

14. It converts alternating current (AC) to low-voltage DC power for the internal components of the computer.
   (A) Optical drive
   (B) Hard disk
   (C) Sound card
   (D) Power supply

15. Power supply are rated by
   (A) Voltage
   (B) Ampere
   (C) Wattage
   (D) Joules

16. It allows the computer to send graphical information to a video display device such as a monitor, TV, or projector.
   (A) Graphic card
   (B) Sound card
   (C) NIC
   (D) DVD

17. The hard disk drive is usually referred to as the
   (A) D drive
   (B) A drive
   (C) B drive
   (D) C drive

18. It connects a computer to a network; such as a home network, or the Internet using an Ethernet cable with an RJ-45 connector.
   (A) Sound card
   (B) Video card
   (C) NIC
   (D) Graphic card

19. It gives you a few days to try the software before you buy the program.
   (A) Freeware
   (B) Hardware
   (C) Open source software
   (D) Shareware

20. Before installing a program in MS-DOS,
   (A) Switch directory that contains the installation files.
   (B) Restart the computer
   (C) Reboot the computer
   (D) Save all the files

21. The foundation of fifth-generation computers is:
    - (A) Artificial Intelligence
    - (B) Vacuum tubes
    - (C) VVLSI
    - (D) Transistors

22. Which of the following is not a software package for an application?
    - (A) Red Hat Linux
    - (B) Adobe Pagemaker
    - (C) Open office
    - (D) All of these
    - (E) None of these

23. Which of the subsequent claims is false?
    - (A) Adobe Photoshop is a program for graphic design.
    - (B) Linux is a free, open-source operating system.
    - (C) Microsoft owns and sells Linux.
    - (D) One such operating system is Windows XP.

24. Which of the following does magnetic disc storage not provide as a benefit?
    - (A) Compared to magnetic tape, magnetic disc has a substantially faster access time.
    - (B) Tape storage costs more than disc storage.
    - (C) Magnetic tape is less durable than disc storage.
    - (D) None of these

25. Which protocol provides an email facility among the hosts?
    - (A) POP
    - (B) SMTP
    - (C) IMAP
    - (D) MIME

Darken Your Choice with HB Pencil

1.	Ⓐ Ⓑ Ⓒ Ⓓ	6.	Ⓐ Ⓑ Ⓒ Ⓓ	11.	Ⓐ Ⓑ Ⓒ Ⓓ	16.	Ⓐ Ⓑ Ⓒ Ⓓ	21.	Ⓐ Ⓑ Ⓒ Ⓓ
2.	Ⓐ Ⓑ Ⓒ Ⓓ	7.	Ⓐ Ⓑ Ⓒ Ⓓ	12.	Ⓐ Ⓑ Ⓒ Ⓓ	17.	Ⓐ Ⓑ Ⓒ Ⓓ	22.	Ⓐ Ⓑ Ⓒ Ⓓ
3.	Ⓐ Ⓑ Ⓒ Ⓓ	8.	Ⓐ Ⓑ Ⓒ Ⓓ	13.	Ⓐ Ⓑ Ⓒ Ⓓ	18.	Ⓐ Ⓑ Ⓒ Ⓓ	23.	Ⓐ Ⓑ Ⓒ Ⓓ
4.	Ⓐ Ⓑ Ⓒ Ⓓ	9.	Ⓐ Ⓑ Ⓒ Ⓓ	14.	Ⓐ Ⓑ Ⓒ Ⓓ	19.	Ⓐ Ⓑ Ⓒ Ⓓ	24.	Ⓐ Ⓑ Ⓒ Ⓓ
5.	Ⓐ Ⓑ Ⓒ Ⓓ	10.	Ⓐ Ⓑ Ⓒ Ⓓ	15.	Ⓐ Ⓑ Ⓒ Ⓓ	20.	Ⓐ Ⓑ Ⓒ Ⓓ	25.	Ⓐ Ⓑ Ⓒ Ⓓ

LEARNING OBJECTIVES

- ➤ Basic input devices
- ➤ Main output devices
- ➤ Different storage types

MULTIPLE CHOICE QUESTIONS

1. Which of the following input devices would be best suited to capture images for use with a personal computer?
   (A) Optical mark reader
   (B) Digital camera
   (C) Touch screen
   (D) Graphics tablet

2. Which output device is suited to present information that is likely to change very frequently?
   (A) Monitor   (B) Plotter
   (C) Printer   (D) Sound card

3. Which of the following might be used to input and interpret information printed on bank cheques?
   (A) MICR   (B) OMR
   (C) CAD   (D) OCR

4. Which type of printer works using a charged drum to deposit particles of ink on the paper?
   (A) Dot-matrix printer
   (B) Inkjet printer
   (C) Daisywheel printer
   (D) Thermal printer

5. Which of the following storage devices is suited to hold large volumes of data that is unlikely to change often?
   (A) Hard disk
   (B) Magnetic tape
   (C) CD-ROM
   (D) Floppy disk

6. Which of the following storage devices is normally used to store the computer's operating system, application software and data?
   (A) CD-ROM
   (B) Magnetic tape
   (C) Hard disk
   (D) Floppy disk

7. In terms of computer storage, which of the following represents the largest unit of measurement?
   (A) Bit
   (B) Byte
   (C) Gigabyte (Gb)
   (D) Kilobyte (Kb)

8. The concept of "zero administration" is associated with:
   (A) PDAs and organisers
   (B) Mini computers
   (C) Desktop computers
   (D) Portable computers

9. The hardware component used to control the operation of a computer system is:
(A) Monitor
(B) Processor
(C) Keyboard
(D) Hard-disk

10. The hardware component used for temporary storage of data and applications for processing is:
(A) Processor
(B) RAM
(C) Hard-disk
(D) Monitor

11. Ali wants to send soft copy of his ID card to passport office online but he only has a desktop computer, which devices does he need to complete this process?
(A) LAN card and Scanner
(B) Card Reader and LAN card
(C) Camera
(D) LAN card

12. Mr. Imran wants to install a security system in his office; what kind of input devices will he require?
(A) Fingerprint Scanner/reader
(B) Camera
(C) OCR
(D) OMR

13. Which one of the following devices uses a laser beam to read and interpret bar code?
(A) Voice input system
(B) Barcode reader
(C) Touch screen
(D) Joystick

14. Which of the following output device(s) provide hardcopy?
(A) Dot matrix printer
(B) Daisy wheel printer
(C) Inkjet printer
(D) All of these

15. Which one of the following is a type of mouse?
(A) Mechanical mouse
(B) Serial mouse
(C) Optical mouse
(D) All of these

16. The device having different types of keys on it is called
(A) Monitor
(B) Keyboard
(C) Trackball
(D) Scanner

17. Which device has a ball beneath it for the rotation?
(A) Trackball
(B) Lightpen
(C) Mouse
(D) Scanner

18. Which device converts any type of printed information into digital pulses?
(A) Plotter
(B) Scanner
(C) Keyboard
(D) Printer

19. Which device has a ball on it that can be spinned in various directions?
(A) Mouse
(B) Scanner
(C) Trackball
(D) Joystick

20. Which device is used to draw lines or figures on a computer screen?
(A) Light pen
(B) Joystick
(C) Trackball
(D) Scanner

21. What kind of thing is a daisy wheel?
    (A) Printer
    (B) Storage device
    (C) Pointing device
    (D) None of these

22. A tool for altering the configuration of a connector's connection is:
    (A) A Converter
    (B) A Component
    (C) An Adapter
    (D) Voltmeter

23. Travel agents use the following computer system while booking flights?
    (A) Supercomputer
    (B) Mainframe computer
    (C) Personal computer
    (D) None of these

24. Registers that are used to hold conditional and are only partially visible to users are known as:
    (A) PC
    (B) General purpose register
    (C) Memory address registers
    (D) Flags

25. Magnetic tapes are suitable for use as a storage material for?
    (A) backup and low volume data
    (B) storing original but low-volume data
    (C) storing original but high-volume data
    (D) backup and high-volume data

Darken Your Choice with HB Pencil

1.	Ⓐ Ⓑ Ⓒ Ⓓ	6.	Ⓐ Ⓑ Ⓒ Ⓓ	11.	Ⓐ Ⓑ Ⓒ Ⓓ	16.	Ⓐ Ⓑ Ⓒ Ⓓ	21.	Ⓐ Ⓑ Ⓒ Ⓓ
2.	Ⓐ Ⓑ Ⓒ Ⓓ	7.	Ⓐ Ⓑ Ⓒ Ⓓ	12.	Ⓐ Ⓑ Ⓒ Ⓓ	17.	Ⓐ Ⓑ Ⓒ Ⓓ	22.	Ⓐ Ⓑ Ⓒ Ⓓ
3.	Ⓐ Ⓑ Ⓒ Ⓓ	8.	Ⓐ Ⓑ Ⓒ Ⓓ	13.	Ⓐ Ⓑ Ⓒ Ⓓ	18.	Ⓐ Ⓑ Ⓒ Ⓓ	23.	Ⓐ Ⓑ Ⓒ Ⓓ
4.	Ⓐ Ⓑ Ⓒ Ⓓ	9.	Ⓐ Ⓑ Ⓒ Ⓓ	14.	Ⓐ Ⓑ Ⓒ Ⓓ	19.	Ⓐ Ⓑ Ⓒ Ⓓ	24.	Ⓐ Ⓑ Ⓒ Ⓓ
5.	Ⓐ Ⓑ Ⓒ Ⓓ	10.	Ⓐ Ⓑ Ⓒ Ⓓ	15.	Ⓐ Ⓑ Ⓒ Ⓓ	20.	Ⓐ Ⓑ Ⓒ Ⓓ	25.	Ⓐ Ⓑ Ⓒ Ⓓ

INTRODUCTION TO HTML AND CS6

LEARNING OBJECTIVES

➤ Basics of HTML
➤ Main HTML Tags

MULTIPLE CHOICE QUESTIONS

1. Choose the correct HTML tag to make a text italic.
   (A) <i>
   (B) <italic>
   (C) <text style="italic">
   (D) <i text="italic">

2. Who is making the Web standards?
   (A) Google
   (B) Intel
   (C) The World Wide Web Consortium
   (D) Microsoft

3. Which of these tags are all <table> tags?
   (A) <table><head><div>
   (B) <table><tr><td>
   (C) <table><tr><li>
   (D) <thead><ul><tr>

4. How can you create an e-mail link?
   (A) <mail>test@google.com</mail>
   (B) <mail href="test@google.com">
   (C) <a href="test@google.com">
   (D) <a href="mailto: test@google.com">

5. How can you open a link in a new browser window?
   (A) <a href="url" target="new">
   (B) <link href="url" target="_blank">
   (C) <a href="url" new>
   (D) <a href="url" target="_blank">

6. What is the correct HTML for inserting an image?
   (A) <img href="imgName.gif" alt="img text"/>
   (B) <img src="imgName.gif" alt="img text"/>
   (C) <img alt="img text"> imgName.gif</img>
   (D) <image src="imgName.gif" alt="img text"/>

7. What is the correct HTML for inserting a background image?
   (A) <background img="bgImgName.gif">
   (B) <imgsrc="bgImgName.gif" background/>
   (C) <body background="bgImgName.gif">
   (D) <bgImgName.gif>

8. What is the correct HTML for making a checkbox?
   (A) <checks>
   (B) <input type="checkbox"/>
   (C) <input type="check"/>
   (D) <checkbox>

9. What is the correct HTML for making a text input field?
   (A) <textinput type="text"/>
   (B) <input type="textfield"/>
   (C) <text type="inputfield"/>
   (D) <input type="text"/>

10. What is the correct HTML for making a drop-down list?
    (A) <input type="dropdown"/>
    (B) <select>
    (C) <input type="dropdown"/>
    (D) <list type="dropdown">
11. Encircle the odd HTML tag
    (A) table
    (B) tr
    (C) td
    (D) form
12. The first page of a website is called
    (A) Design page
    (B) Home page
    (C) First page
    (D) Main page
13. The version of HTML is?
    (A) HTML 0
    (B) HTML 1
    (C) HTML 2
    (D) All of these
14. There are how many Heading Tags
    (A) 3
    (B) 4
    (C) 5
    (D) 6
15. Which is the largest Heading Tag?
    (A) H1
    (B) H3
    (C) H4
    (D) H6

16. Which of the following are attributes of Font Tag?
    (A) Face
    (B) Size
    (C) Colour
    (D) All of these
17. There are how many types of lists in HTML?
    (A) 1
    (B) 2
    (C) 3
    (D) 6
18. Which of the following is used to increase the row height?
    (A) Cells pacing
    (B) Cell padding
    (C) Row span
    (D) Height property with <tr> tag
19. Which of the following is used to increase the col width?
    (A) Cell spacing
    (B) Cell padding
    (C) Width attribute in the <td> tag
    (D) Col span
20. Which one of the following is/are invalid tag in HTML?
    (A) <table>
    (B) <caption>
    (C) <colspan>
    (D) </table>

HOTS (ACHIEVERS SECTION)

21. Which of the following is a paired tag?
    (A) <img>
    (B)
    (C) <b>
    (D) <hr>
22. Which of the following is not an attribute of <img> ?
    (A) size
    (B) width
    (C) alt
    (D) src
23. Which tag is used to scroll the text in the specified direction?
    (A) Scroll
    (B) Animate
    (C) Movingtext
    (D) Marquee

24. What is the correct HTML code for making a hyperlink?

(A) <a url =?http//www.xxxx.com?>xxxxx.com>/a>

(B) <a name=?http://www.xxxx.com?>xxxxx.com</a>

(C) <a>http://www.xxxx.com</a>

(D) <a href =?http://www.xxxx.com?>xxxx</a>

25. Varun has been given an assignment to write HTML code for the creation of table. But he made a mistake in his program. What is the correction of his error?

<HTML> <HEAD> <TITLE> creating a table </TITLE> <BODY> <TABLE BORDER = "5" WIDTH = "100%"> <TR> <TH> class </TH> <TH> time </TH> <TR> <TD> computer science </TD> <TD> 10:00 </TD> </TR> </TABLE> </BODY> </HTML>

(A) After giving the headings OFF the <TR> tag.

(B) The OFF tag for <HEAD> should be given at the end.

(C) The OFF tag for <BODY> should be given after the <TABLE> tag.

(D) The attributes of table should be defined separately.

1.	A B C D	6.	A B C D	11.	A B C D	16.	A B C D	21.	A B C D
2.	A B C D	7.	A B C D	12.	A B C D	17.	A B C D	22.	A B C D
3.	A B C D	8.	A B C D	13.	A B C D	18.	A B C D	23.	A B C D
4.	A B C D	9.	A B C D	14.	A B C D	19.	A B C D	24.	A B C D
5.	A B C D	10.	A B C D	15.	A B C D	20.	A B C D	25.	A B C D

INTRODUCTION TO FLASH CS6 

MULTIPLE CHOICE QUESTIONS

1. To use oval tool, press
   (A) Y on the keyboard
   (B) L on the keyboard
   (C) R on the keyboard
   (D) O on the keyboard

2. To use line tool, press
   (A) N on the keyboard
   (B) L on the keyboard
   (C) R on the keyboard
   (D) O on the keyboard

3. To use rectangle tool, press
   (A) Y on the keyboard
   (B) L on the keyboard
   (C) R on the keyboard
   (D) O on the keyboard

4. The default width of line tool is
   (A) 2 Pt
   (B) 3 Pt
   (C) 1 Pt
   (D) 1.5 Pt

5. This tool helps you to draw four-sided shapes.
   (A) Oval tool
   (B) Line tool
   (C) Rectangle tool
   (D) Pencil tool

6. This tool helps you to draw free hand.
   (A) Oval tool
   (B) Line tool
   (C) Rectangle tool
   (D) Pencil tool

7. This tool helps you to erase a portion of your drawing.
   (A) Oval tool
   (B) Eraser tool
   (C) Rectangle tool
   (D) Pencil tool

8. This tool helps you to draw straight lines
   (A) Oval tool
   (B) Line tool
   (C) Rectangle tool
   (D) Pencil tool

9. This tool helps you to draw curved lines.
   (A) Oval tool
   (B) Line tool
   (C) Rectangle tool
   (D) Pencil tool

10. Pressing Ctrl + N will
    (A) open a new file
    (B) Save a file

(C) exit a document

(D) delete a document

11. Pressing Ctrl + Q will

(A) open a new file

(B) Save a file

(C) exit a document

(D) delete a document

12. Pressing ALT + F4 will

(A) open a new file

(B) Save a file

(C) exit a document

(D) delete a document

13. Timeline

(A) displays a set of frames that are used to create animation.

(B) is a set of tools used to create images on Flash.

(C) displays options that you can use in Flash.

(D) is the drawing area where images are created.

14. Stage

(A) displays a set of frames that are used to create animation.

(B) is a set of tools used to create images on Flash.

(C) displays options that you can use in Flash.

(D) is the drawing area where images are created.

15. Adobe Flash CS6 was launched in

(A) 2010

(B) 2011

(C) 2012

(D) 2014

HOTS (ACHIEVERS SECTION)

16. Use this to move symbols from one point to another. All animation happens between key frames (point A and B). The timeline turns purple between the key frames when this feature is being used. A dashed or dotted line in the colored area indicates a problem.

(A) Motion Tween   (B) Mask

(C) Shape Tween   (D) Action Script

17. Use this to make a symbol disappear from view (great for changing pictures). You would use motion tween for this method. You have to change the "alpha" setting of the symbol. Alpha represents transparency.

(A) Zoom

(B) Masking

(C) Fade Effect

(D) Morphing

18. What is a Blank Keyframe?

(A) A frame that is the same as the keyframe before it – it looks like a gray rectangle without a dot

(B) A frame that represents a change in content, be that scale, movement, rotation, color, etc – it looks like a gray rectangle with a black dot

(C) A frame without any content – it looks like a white box

(D) A frame without any content – it looks like a white box with a white dot

19. To apply a stroke to a shape that does not currently have one, you;

(A) Select the shape, open the dialogue box in the properties window for ink color and make a selection. From there you can edit the weight and style in the properties window.

(B) Select the ink tool in the tool box, select the ink color in the color picker and click on the shape near the outside of its fill. From there you can edit the weight and style in the properties window.

(C) Select the paint bucket in the tool box, select the ink color in the color picker and click on the shape near the outside of its fill. From there you can edit the weight and style in the properties window.

(D) Go to the actions window and add the "addStroke()" method to the fill. Be sure to also set the "strokeColor" and "strokeWeight" properties.

20. The difference between the black arrow and the white arrow in the tool box is;

(A) The black arrow allows us to manipulate the shape as a whole by repositioning it on the stage or fluidly transforming its shape by selecting the curves that define it and repositioning those. The white arrow allows us to have more precise control of the points that define the shape by allowing us to manipulate their anchor points and beizier curves.

(B) The black arrow allows us to manipulate the shape as a whole by repositioning it on the stage or fluidly transforming its shape by selecting the curves that define it and repositioning those. The white arrow allows us to transform the shape by scaling, rotating, skewing and distorting it.

(C) The white arrow allows us to manipulate the shape as a whole by repositioning it on the stage or fluidly transforming its shape by selecting the curves that define it and repositioning those. The black arrow allows us to have more precise control of the points that define the shape by allowing us to manipulate their anchor points and beizier curves.

(D) The white arrow allows us to manipulate the shape as a whole by repositioning it on the stage or fluidly transforming its shape by selecting the curves that define it and repositioning those. The black arrow allows us to transform the shape by scaling, rotating, skewing and distorting it.

	A B C D		A B C D		A B C D		A B C D		A B C D
1.	Ⓐ Ⓑ Ⓒ Ⓓ	5.	Ⓐ Ⓑ Ⓒ Ⓓ	9.	Ⓐ Ⓑ Ⓒ Ⓓ	13.	Ⓐ Ⓑ Ⓒ Ⓓ	17.	Ⓐ Ⓑ Ⓒ Ⓓ
2.	Ⓐ Ⓑ Ⓒ Ⓓ	6.	Ⓐ Ⓑ Ⓒ Ⓓ	10.	Ⓐ Ⓑ Ⓒ Ⓓ	14.	Ⓐ Ⓑ Ⓒ Ⓓ	18.	Ⓐ Ⓑ Ⓒ Ⓓ
3.	Ⓐ Ⓑ Ⓒ Ⓓ	7.	Ⓐ Ⓑ Ⓒ Ⓓ	11.	Ⓐ Ⓑ Ⓒ Ⓓ	15.	Ⓐ Ⓑ Ⓒ Ⓓ	19.	Ⓐ Ⓑ Ⓒ Ⓓ
4.	Ⓐ Ⓑ Ⓒ Ⓓ	8.	Ⓐ Ⓑ Ⓒ Ⓓ	12.	Ⓐ Ⓑ Ⓒ Ⓓ	16.	Ⓐ Ⓑ Ⓒ Ⓓ	20.	Ⓐ Ⓑ Ⓒ Ⓓ

MS WORD

5

LEARNING OBJECTIVES

➤ Basic concepts of MS Word
➤ Working with MS Word

MULTIPLE CHOICE QUESTIONS

1. MS Word is used for
   (A) Drawing pictures
   (B) Doing calculations
   (C) Typing letters
   (D) Creating animations
2. MS Word comes as part of the
   (A) MS Office tools   (B) MS Home tools
   (C) MS Outdoor tools (D) MS Acess tools
3. MS Word has the file extension
   (A) .htm   (B) .fla
   (C) .sav   (D) .doc
4. Pressing Ctrl + F
   (A) Opens the Find Dialog box
   (B) Saves the document
   (C) Deletes the document
   (D) Replaces the document
5. Pressing Ctrl + H
   (A) Opens the find what box
   (B) Saves the document
   (C) Replaces a word or phrase in the document
   (D) Replaces the document
6. Verdana is a type of
   (A) Font size   (B) Font style
   (C) Font colour   (D) Font effect
7. Pressing Ctrl + U
   (A) Makes the text bold
   (B) Makes the text italics
   (C) Makes the text underlined
   (D) Deletes the text
8. The title bar does not have this button.
   (A) Maximize   (B) Minimize
   (C) Close   (D) Insert
9. 2/10 on the status bar means
   (A) Tenth page of two pages
   (B) Second page of ten pages
   (C) Second line of ten pages
   (D) Second line of ten lines
10. Left arrow key
    (A) Moves cursor one space to the right
    (B) Moves cursor one space to the left
    (C) Moves cursor up
    (D) Moves cursor down
11. Home key
    (A) Moves cursor to the right
    (B) Moves cursor to the end of the line
    (C) Moves cursor to the beginning of the line
    (D) Move cursor to the end of the page
12. A paragraph is made by pressing the
    (A) Shift key   (B) Ctrl key
    (C) Enter key   (D) Alt key
13. WordArt is used to insert
    (A) Shapes   (B) Images
    (C) Decorative text   (D) Animation
14. What happens if you check match case in Find what box?
    (A) It finds only those words that match the case
    (B) It finds all the words with the same spelling
    (C) It does not find words that match the case
    (D) It does not find any word at all

15. Clipart can be inserted from the
    (A) View menu   (B) Edit menu
    (C) Insert menu   (D) Home menu
16. Who is the owner of MicroSoft?
    (A) Mark Zuckerberg (B) Bill Gates
    (C) Anil Ambani   (D) Steve Jobs
17. Bold, underline and italics
    (A) Can be used manually only
    (B) Have toggle buttons
    (C) Do not have toggle buttons
    (D) Cannot be used in MS Word
18. Toggle buttons are like
    (A) ON and OFF switch
    (B) Options on the menu bar
    (C) Options under the file menu
    (D) List of options on the drop down menu
19. Redo button can be used only after you use
    (A) Copy paste option (B) Undo button
    (C) Cut option   (D) Insert option
20. The insertion point is in the shape of a/an
    (A) L beam   (B) I beam
    (C) T beam   (D) J beam

HOTS (ACHIEVERS SECTION)

21. You wished to justify text over the height of paper, which option will you choose
    (A) Page Setup from File menu
    (B) Paragraph from Format menu
    (C) From formatting toolbar
    (D) Font from Format menu
22. On which toolbar can you find Format Painter tool?
    (A) Standard toolbar
    (B) Formatting toolbar
    (C) Drawing Toolbar
    (D) Picture Toolbar
23. Which function allows you to type straight quotations in place of smart quotes?
    (A) Auto Correct as you type
    (B) Auto Change as you type
    (C) Auto Ignore as you type
    (D) Auto Format as you type
24. What does Ctrl + G do?
    (A) Goto Tab is activated while the Find and Replace dialogue box is opened.
    (B) With the Find Tab selected, launch the Find and Replace dialogue box.
    (C) Activate the Replace tab to open the Find and Replace dialogue box.
    (D) Launch the Goto Dialog box
25. Shortcut Ctrl +H is used for:
    (A) Activate the Insert Hyper Link Tab by opening the Insert Dialog box.
    (B) Activate the Find and Replace dialogue box to display Access Tab
    (C) With the Find Tab selected, launch the Find and Replace dialogue box.
    (D) Opens the find and replace tool that lets you search for a character, word or phrase and replace it with something else.

—Darken Your Choice with HB Pencil—

	A B C D		A B C D		A B C D		A B C D		A B C D
1.	Ⓐ Ⓑ Ⓒ Ⓓ	6.	Ⓐ Ⓑ Ⓒ Ⓓ	11.	Ⓐ Ⓑ Ⓒ Ⓓ	16.	Ⓐ Ⓑ Ⓒ Ⓓ	21.	Ⓐ Ⓑ Ⓒ Ⓓ
2.	Ⓐ Ⓑ Ⓒ Ⓓ	7.	Ⓐ Ⓑ Ⓒ Ⓓ	12.	Ⓐ Ⓑ Ⓒ Ⓓ	17.	Ⓐ Ⓑ Ⓒ Ⓓ	22.	Ⓐ Ⓑ Ⓒ Ⓓ
3.	Ⓐ Ⓑ Ⓒ Ⓓ	8.	Ⓐ Ⓑ Ⓒ Ⓓ	13.	Ⓐ Ⓑ Ⓒ Ⓓ	18.	Ⓐ Ⓑ Ⓒ Ⓓ	23.	Ⓐ Ⓑ Ⓒ Ⓓ
4.	Ⓐ Ⓑ Ⓒ Ⓓ	9.	Ⓐ Ⓑ Ⓒ Ⓓ	14.	Ⓐ Ⓑ Ⓒ Ⓓ	19.	Ⓐ Ⓑ Ⓒ Ⓓ	24.	Ⓐ Ⓑ Ⓒ Ⓓ
5.	Ⓐ Ⓑ Ⓒ Ⓓ	10.	Ⓐ Ⓑ Ⓒ Ⓓ	15.	Ⓐ Ⓑ Ⓒ Ⓓ	20.	Ⓐ Ⓑ Ⓒ Ⓓ	25.	Ⓐ Ⓑ Ⓒ Ⓓ

LEARNING OBJECTIVES

➤ Basic concepts of MS PowerPoint
➤ Working with MS PowerPoint

MULTIPLE CHOICE QUESTIONS

1. Which file format can be added to a PowerPoint show?
   (A) .jpg
   (B) .giv
   (C) .wav
   (D) All of these

2. In Microsoft PowerPoint two kind of sound effects files that can be added to the presentation are:
   (A) .wav files and .mid files
   (B) .wav files and .gif files
   (C) .wav files and .jpg files
   (D) .jpg files and .gif files

3. What is a motion path?
   (A) A type of animation entrance effect
   (B) A method of advancing slides
   (C) A method of moving items on a slide
   (D) All of these

4. What is a slide-title master pair?
   (A) The title area and text area of a specific slide
   (B) A slide master and title master merged into a single slide
   (C) A slide master and title master for a specific design template
   (D) All of these

5. Which of the following should you use if you want all the slide in the presentation to have the same "look"?
   (A) The slide layout option
   (B) Add a slide option
   (C) Outline view
   (D) A presentation design template

6. In the context of animations, what is a trigger?
   (A) An action button that advances to the next slide
   (B) An item on the slide that performs an action when clicked
   (C) The name of a motion path
   (D) All of these

7. To exit PowerPoint
   (A) Click the application minimize button
   (B) Click the document close button
   (C) Double click the applications control menu icon
   (D) Double click the document control menu icon

8. To preview a motion path effect using the custom animation task pane, you should
   (A) Click the play button
   (B) Click the show effect button
   (C) Double click the motion path
   (D) All of these

9. You can create a new presentation by completing all of the following except
(A) Clicking the New button on the standard toolbar
(B) Clicking File, New
(C) Clicking File, Open
(D) Pressing Ctrl + N

10. To select one hyperlink after another during a slide presentation, what do you press?
(A) Tab
(B) Ctrl + K
(C) Ctrl + H
(D) All of these

11. Special effects used to introduce slides in a presentation are called
(A) Effects
(B) Custom animations
(C) Transitions
(D) Present animations

12. You can edit an embedded organization chart object by
(A) Clicking edit object
(B) Double clicking the organization chart object
(C) Right clicking the chart object, then clicking edit MS-Organization Chart object
(D) Both (B) and (C)

13. What is the term used when you press and hold the left mouse key and more the mouse around the slide?
(A) Highlighting
(B) Dragging
(C) Selecting
(D) Moving

14. Which of the following toolbars provide different options in various master views?
(A) Common tasks toolbar
(B) Drawing toolbar
(C) Formatting toolbar
(D) Standard toolbar

15. How can you create a uniform appearance by adding a background image to all slides?
(A) Create a template
(B) Edit the slide master
(C) Use the autocorrect wizard
(D) All of these

16. Which key on the keyboard can be used to view Slide show?
(A) F1
(B) F2
(C) F5
(D) F10

17. Which view in Power Point can be used to enter Speaker Comments?
(A) Normal
(B) Slide Show
(C) Slide Sorter
(D) Notes Page view

18. Which option can be used to create a new slide show with the current slides but presented in a different order?
(A) Rehearsal
(B) Custom Slide show
(C) Slide Show Setup
(D) Slide Show View

19. The boxes that are displayed to indicate that the text, pictures or objects are placed in it is called ________
(A) Placeholder
(B) AutoText
(C) Text box
(D) Word Art

20. Which type of fonts are best suited for titles and headlines?
(A) Serif Fonts
(B) Sans Serif Fonts
(C) Text Fonts
(D) Picture Fonts

21. Which of the following alignment cannot be placed where the tab stops?
    (A) Decimal Alignment
    (B) Center Alignment
    (C) Bar Alignment
    (D) Justify Alignment

22. In Microsoft PowerPoint you have customized a design template in one presentation and you want to use it in another presentation. What the best way to do this?
    (A) Copy and paste the slide with the design template you want to include the new presentation; inserted slide will inherit the design
    (B) Use the browse feature in the slide design task pane to find the file that has your design template and apply it to the current file.
    (C) Save the presentation that has the design template with a new name, and then use a new file to your presentation
    (D) All of these

23. How do you create speaker note pages that show the slides, related notes, and your company logo on each page?
    (A) Edit the slide master and insert your company logo and notes pane
    (B) Edit the notes master and add your company logo
    (C) Edit the handout master to include your company logo and one slide per page with additional note space
    (D) All of these

24. In Microsoft PowerPoint presentation designs regulate the formatting and layout for the slide and are commonly called
    (A) Placeholders
    (B) Design templates
    (C) Blueprints
    (D) Templates

25. In Microsoft PowerPoint the term used to describe the separation of a clip art object into different parts so that it becomes a PowerPoint object
    (A) Ungrouping
    (B) Embedding
    (C) Grouping
    (D) Regrouping

Darken Your Choice with HB Pencil

1.	Ⓐ Ⓑ Ⓒ Ⓓ	6.	Ⓐ Ⓑ Ⓒ Ⓓ	11.	Ⓐ Ⓑ Ⓒ Ⓓ	16.	Ⓐ Ⓑ Ⓒ Ⓓ	21.	Ⓐ Ⓑ Ⓒ Ⓓ
2.	Ⓐ Ⓑ Ⓒ Ⓓ	7.	Ⓐ Ⓑ Ⓒ Ⓓ	12.	Ⓐ Ⓑ Ⓒ Ⓓ	17.	Ⓐ Ⓑ Ⓒ Ⓓ	22.	Ⓐ Ⓑ Ⓒ Ⓓ
3.	Ⓐ Ⓑ Ⓒ Ⓓ	8.	Ⓐ Ⓑ Ⓒ Ⓓ	13.	Ⓐ Ⓑ Ⓒ Ⓓ	18.	Ⓐ Ⓑ Ⓒ Ⓓ	23.	Ⓐ Ⓑ Ⓒ Ⓓ
4.	Ⓐ Ⓑ Ⓒ Ⓓ	9.	Ⓐ Ⓑ Ⓒ Ⓓ	14.	Ⓐ Ⓑ Ⓒ Ⓓ	19.	Ⓐ Ⓑ Ⓒ Ⓓ	24.	Ⓐ Ⓑ Ⓒ Ⓓ
5.	Ⓐ Ⓑ Ⓒ Ⓓ	10.	Ⓐ Ⓑ Ⓒ Ⓓ	15.	Ⓐ Ⓑ Ⓒ Ⓓ	20.	Ⓐ Ⓑ Ⓒ Ⓓ	25.	Ⓐ Ⓑ Ⓒ Ⓓ

MS EXCEL

LEARNING OBJECTIVES

➤ Basic concepts of MS Excel
➤ Working with MS Excel
➤ Data Types, Formulas and Functions

MULTIPLE CHOICE QUESTIONS

1. What function displays row data in a column or column data in a row?
   (A) Hyperlink (B) Index
   (C) Transpose (D) Rows

2. Except for the _______ function, a formula with a logical function shows the word "TRUE" or "FALSE" as a result
   (A) IF (B) AND
   (C) OR (D) NOT

3. Each excel file is called a workbook because
   (A) It can contain text and data
   (B) It can be modified
   (C) It can contain many sheets including worksheets and chart sheets
   (D) You have to work hard to create it

4. Which types of charts can excel produce?
   (A) Line graphs and pie charts only
   (B) Only line graphs
   (C) Bar charts, line graphs and pie charts
   (D) Bar charts and line graphs only

5. How are data organized in a spreadsheet?
   (A) Lines and spaces
   (B) Layers and planes
   (C) Rows and columns
   (D) Height and width

6. Which of the following is a correct order of precedence in a formula calculation?
   (A) Multiplication and division, exponential positive and negative value
   (B) Multiplication and division, positive and negative values, addition and subtraction
   (C) Addition and subtraction, positive and negative values, exponentiation
   (D) None of these

7. How should you print a selected area of a worksheet, if you want to print a different area next time?
   (A) On the file menu, point to print area, and then click set print area.
   (B) On the file menu, click print, and then click selection under print what
   (C) On the view menu, click custom views, then click add
   (D) All of these

8. Which of the following methods can not be used to enter data in a cell?
   (A) Pressing an arrow key
   (B) Pressing the tab key
   (C) Pressing the Esc key
   (D) Clicking the enter button to the formula bar

9. Which of the following methods cannot be used to edit the content of cell?
   (A) Pressing the Alt key
   (B) Clicking the formula bar
   (C) Pressing F2
   (D) Double clicking the cell

10. You can activate a cell by
   (A) Pressing the Tab key
   (B) Clicking the cell
   (C) Pressing an arrow key
   (D) All of these

11. Which of the following describes how to select all the cells in a single column?
   (A) Right click on column and select Pick from list
   (B) Use data – text to columns menu item
   (C) Left click on the gray column title button
   (D) Pressing Ctrl + A on the keyboard

12. Paper spreadsheets can have all the same advantages as an electronic spreadsheet except which of the following?
   (A) Rows and columns
   (B) Headings
   (C) Speed
   (D) None

13. Which of the following is not a basic step in creating a worksheet?
   (A) Save the workbook
   (B) Modify the worksheet
   (C) Enter text and data
   (D) Copy the worksheet

14. To insert three columns between columns D and E you would
   (A) Select column D
   (B) Select column E
   (C) Select columns E, F and G
   (D) Select columns D, E, and F

15. Charts tips can
   (A) Show the formatting of a data label
   (B) Show the name of a data series
   (C) Show the value of data point
   (D) Both (B) and (C)

16. How do you change column width to fit the contents?
   (A) Single-click the boundary to the left to the column heading
   (B) Double click the boundary to the right of the column heading
   (C) Press Alt and single click anywhere in the column
   (D) All of these

17. You can use the horizontal and vertical scroll bars to
   (A) Split a worksheet into two panes
   (B) View different rows and columns
   (C) Edit the contents of a cell
   (D) View different worksheets

18. To drag a selected range of data to another worksheet in the same workbook, use the
   (A) Tab key
   (B) Alt key
   (C) Shift key
   (D) Ctrl key

19. When the formula bar is activated, you can see
   (A) The Edit Formula button
   (B) The Cancel button
   (C) The Enter button
   (D) All of these

20. In a worksheet you can select
   (A) The entire worksheet
   (B) Rows
   (C) Columns
   (D) (A), (B), and (C)

21. When you link data maintained in an excel workbook to a word document
    (A) The word document cannot be edited
    (B) The word document contains a reference to the original source application
    (C) The word document must contain a hyperlink
    (D) The word document contains a copy of the actual data

22. To edit in an embedded excel worksheet object in a word document
    (A) Use the excel menu bar and toolbars inside the word application
    (B) Edit the hyperlink
    (C) Edit the data in a excel source application
    (D) Use the word menu bar and toolbars

23. Rounding errors can occur
    (A) When you use multiplication, division, or exponentiation in a formula
    (B) When you use addition and subtraction in a formula
    (C) Because excel uses hidden decimal places in computation
    (D) When you show the results of formulas with different decimal places that the calculated results

24. How can you find specific information in a list?
    (A) Select Tools > Finder from the menu
    (B) Click the Find button on the standard toolbar
    (C) Select Insert > Find from the menu
    (D) Select Data > Form from the menu to open the Data Form dialog box and click the Criteria button

25. To center worksheet titles across a range of cells, you must
    (A) Select the cells containing the title text plus the range over which the title text is to be centered
    (B) Widen the columns
    (C) Select the cells containing the title text plus the range over which the title text is to be enfettered
    (D) Format the cells with the comma style

Darken Your Choice with HB Pencil

1.	Ⓐ Ⓑ Ⓒ Ⓓ	6.	Ⓐ Ⓑ Ⓒ Ⓓ	11.	Ⓐ Ⓑ Ⓒ Ⓓ	16.	Ⓐ Ⓑ Ⓒ Ⓓ	21.	Ⓐ Ⓑ Ⓒ Ⓓ
2.	Ⓐ Ⓑ Ⓒ Ⓓ	7.	Ⓐ Ⓑ Ⓒ Ⓓ	12.	Ⓐ Ⓑ Ⓒ Ⓓ	17.	Ⓐ Ⓑ Ⓒ Ⓓ	22.	Ⓐ Ⓑ Ⓒ Ⓓ
3.	Ⓐ Ⓑ Ⓒ Ⓓ	8.	Ⓐ Ⓑ Ⓒ Ⓓ	13.	Ⓐ Ⓑ Ⓒ Ⓓ	18.	Ⓐ Ⓑ Ⓒ Ⓓ	23.	Ⓐ Ⓑ Ⓒ Ⓓ
4.	Ⓐ Ⓑ Ⓒ Ⓓ	9.	Ⓐ Ⓑ Ⓒ Ⓓ	14.	Ⓐ Ⓑ Ⓒ Ⓓ	19.	Ⓐ Ⓑ Ⓒ Ⓓ	24.	Ⓐ Ⓑ Ⓒ Ⓓ
5.	Ⓐ Ⓑ Ⓒ Ⓓ	10.	Ⓐ Ⓑ Ⓒ Ⓓ	15.	Ⓐ Ⓑ Ⓒ Ⓓ	20.	Ⓐ Ⓑ Ⓒ Ⓓ	25.	Ⓐ Ⓑ Ⓒ Ⓓ

PROGRAMMING IN QBASIC

LEARNING OBJECTIVES

➤ Basic concepts of MS Access
➤ Working with Data in MS Access

MULTIPLE CHOICE QUESTIONS

1. Computer based record keeping system is known as
   - (A) CRKS
   - (B) DBMS
   - (C) DMS
   - (D) All of these

2. Duplication of data is known as
   - (A) Data redundancy
   - (B) Data repentance
   - (C) Data inconsistency
   - (D) None of these

3. Multiple copies of same data that mismatch are known as
   - (A) Data redundancy
   - (B) Data repentance
   - (C) Data inconsistency
   - (D) None of these

4. A storage container storing data pertaining to a simple object, subject or purpose is known as
   - (A) Table
   - (B) Query
   - (C) Report
   - (D) Form

5. A field that uniquely identifies record in a table is known as
   - (A) Candidate key
   - (B) Primary key
   - (C) Unique key
   - (D) Special key

6. A statement that gives you filtered data according to your conditions and specifications is called
   - (A) Table
   - (B) Query
   - (C) Report
   - (D) Form

7. An interface in user defined layout that lets the user view enter or change data in tables:
   - (A) Table
   - (B) Query
   - (C) Report
   - (D) Form

8. A formal presentable printed document that lists data in formatted way is known as:
   - (A) Table
   - (B) Query
   - (C) Report
   - (D) Form

9. Named collection of fields which represent a complete unit of information is called:
   (A) Field
   (B) Record
   (C) Table
   (D) None of these

10. DBMS stands for:
   (A) Data Base Management System
   (B) Data Basic Management System
   (C) Data Base Multiple System
   (D) Direct Basic Multiple System

11. What are the different views to display a table
   (A) Datasheet View
   (B) Design View
   (C) Pivot Table & Pivot Chart View
   (D) All of these

12. Which of the following creates a drop down list of values to choose from?
   (A) Ole Object
   (B) Hyperlink
   (C) Memo
   (D) Lookup Wizard

13. The command center of access file that appears when you create or open the ms access database file.
   (A) Database Window
   (B) Query Window
   (C) Design View Window
   (D) Switchboard

14. The third stage in designing a database is when we analyze our tables more closely and create a _________ between tables
   (A) Relationship
   (B) Join
   (C) Query
   (D) None of these

15. What is function of freeze column option?
   (A) Insert a new column
   (B) Insert a new row
   (C) Freeze the selected column
   (D) Deletes a row

16. The "Hyperlink" Data is used to store _______ in MS access
   (A) Web Address
   (B) Path of a File
   (C) email Address
   (D) All of these

17. It is an association established between common fields of two tables
   (A) Line
   (B) Relationship
   (C) Primary Key
   (D) Records

18. This is the stage in database design where one gathers and list all the necessary fields for the database project.
   (A) Data Definition
   (B) Data Refinement
   (C) Establishing Relationship
   (D) None of these

19. A database language concerned with the definition of the whole database structure and schema is _______
   (A) DCL
   (B) DML
   (C) DDL
   (D) All of these

20. Which of the field has width 8 bytes?
   (A) Memo
   (B) Number
   (C) Date/Time
   (D) Hyperlink

21. The filter by selection feature allows you to filter
    (A) Records that meet any of several criteria you specify
    (B) Those records that match an entity in a field
    (C) Records based on a criterion you specify
    (D) All of these

22. In Access press CTRL+F6 to
    (A) Turn on Resize mode for the active window when it is not maximized; press the arrow keys to resize the window
    (B) Restore the selected minimized window when all windows are minimized
    (C) Cycle between open windows
    (D) Toggle the Navigation Pane

23. You can display a database object in design view by
    (A) Selecting the database object and clicking the design button on the database window
    (B) Opening the database object and clicking the view button on the toolbar
    (C) Opening the database object and selecting Tools > Design view
    (D) Selecting the database object and press Ctrl + V

24. Which of the following is not a selection technique ?
    (A) To select a column, double click anywhere in the column
    (B) To select a row, click the record selector box to the left of the row
    (C) To select an entire table click the empty bosx to the left of the field names
    (D) To select a word, double click the word

25. (IF [Age]>65, "Senior","Adult") This expression is an example of:
    (A) A financial expression
    (B) Something that belongs in a Microsoft Excel book
    (C) Algebraic expression
    (D) A conditional expression

Darken Your Choice with HB Pencil

1.	Ⓐ Ⓑ Ⓒ Ⓓ	6.	Ⓐ Ⓑ Ⓒ Ⓓ	11.	Ⓐ Ⓑ Ⓒ Ⓓ	16.	Ⓐ Ⓑ Ⓒ Ⓓ	21.	Ⓐ Ⓑ Ⓒ Ⓓ
2.	Ⓐ Ⓑ Ⓒ Ⓓ	7.	Ⓐ Ⓑ Ⓒ Ⓓ	12.	Ⓐ Ⓑ Ⓒ Ⓓ	17.	Ⓐ Ⓑ Ⓒ Ⓓ	22.	Ⓐ Ⓑ Ⓒ Ⓓ
3.	Ⓐ Ⓑ Ⓒ Ⓓ	8.	Ⓐ Ⓑ Ⓒ Ⓓ	13.	Ⓐ Ⓑ Ⓒ Ⓓ	18.	Ⓐ Ⓑ Ⓒ Ⓓ	23.	Ⓐ Ⓑ Ⓒ Ⓓ
4.	Ⓐ Ⓑ Ⓒ Ⓓ	9.	Ⓐ Ⓑ Ⓒ Ⓓ	14.	Ⓐ Ⓑ Ⓒ Ⓓ	19.	Ⓐ Ⓑ Ⓒ Ⓓ	24.	Ⓐ Ⓑ Ⓒ Ⓓ
5.	Ⓐ Ⓑ Ⓒ Ⓓ	10.	Ⓐ Ⓑ Ⓒ Ⓓ	15.	Ⓐ Ⓑ Ⓒ Ⓓ	20.	Ⓐ Ⓑ Ⓒ Ⓓ	25.	Ⓐ Ⓑ Ⓒ Ⓓ

LEARNING OBJECTIVES

➤ Web and Internet
➤ Network Address

➤ Cyber crime
➤ IT ACT 2000

MULTIPLE CHOICE QUESTIONS

1. Which of the following identifies a specific web page and its computer on the Web?
   (A) Web site
   (B) Web site address
   (C) URL
   (D) Domain Name

2. Which of the following terms applies to all the web pages for amazon.com?
   (A) Top-level domain
   (B) Web site
   (C) Web site address
   (D) Web domain

3. Software, such as Internet Explorer and Firefox, are referred to as ______.
   (A) Systems software
   (B) Utility software
   (C) Browsers
   (D) Internet tools

4. Which of the following ISP's is free?
   (A) CompuServe
   (B) AOL
   (C) NetZero
   (D) MSN

5. If you want to be part of an online community that creates an educational web site which allows its members to add to or change its information, what type of website would you need?
   (A) Educational or .edu
   (B) Social networking site
   (C) Wiki
   (D) Web 2.0

6. If you want to create a broadcast that could be downloaded from the Internet, what would you create?
   (A) IBroadcast
   (B) EShow
   (C) Podcast
   (D) ICast

7. When data moves from one set of major connections to another on the Internet, we call these connections the Internet ______.
   (A) Pathway
   (B) Backbone
   (C) Communications system
   (D) Routers

8. When internet data leaves your campus, it normally goes to a(n) ______ before moving toward its destination.
   (A) Internet backbone
   (B) Network access point
   (C) Base station
   (D) Communication system

9. MCI and AT&T are examples of which of the following?
(A) Social networks
(B) Communications systems
(C) Internet service providers
(D) Mobisodes

10. What type of telecommunications hardware allows you to access the web?
(A) Browser
(B) Modem
(C) FTP protocol
(D) IRC

11. TCP/IP is a:
(A) Network Hardware
(B) Network Software
(C) Protocol
(D) None of these

12. OSI stands for:
(A) Open System Interface
(B) Out System Interface
(C) Open System Interconnection
(D) Out System Interconnection

13. TCP/IP is mainly used for:
(A) File Transfer
(B) Email
(C) Remote Login Service
(D) All of these

14. Which of the following is a chatting application?
(A) WhatsApp
(B) Google earth
(C) You-tube
(D) None of these

15 Which of the following is a threat for clients?
(A) Virus
(B) Worms
(C) Trojan Horses
(D) All of these

16 Which of the following is not an application of internet?
(A) Communication
(B) Banking
(C) Shopping
(D) Sleeping

17. Which is the advantage of e-business?
(A) Better Service
(B) Reduction of cost
(C) Reduction of paper work
(D) All of these

18. Internet's initial development was supported by
(A) ARPANET
(B) Bill Rogers
(C) Bill Gates
(D) Microsoft

19. World Wide Web was proposed by?
(A) Bill Gates
(B) ARPANET
(C) Tim Berners-Lee
(D) Bill Rogers

20. What is the full form of URL?
(A) Uniform Resource Library
(B) Uniform Resource Locator
(C) United Resource Library
(D) United Resource Locators

21. Which of the following virus overtake computer system, when it boots and destroy information?
    (A) System infectors
    (B) Trojan
    (C) Boot infectors
    (D) Stealth virus

22. Which of the following would most likely not be a symptom of a virus?
    (A) The web browser opens to an unusual home page
    (B) Odd message or images are displayed on the screen
    (C) Existing program files and icons disappear
    (D) The CD–ROM stops functioning

23. Which of the following describes programs that can run independently travel from system to system and disrupt computer communication?
    (A) Viruses
    (B) Trojans
    (C) Droppers
    (D) Worm

24. Secret–key encryption is also known as
    (A) Secret–encryption
    (B) Private encryption
    (C) Symmetric encryption
    (D) Asymmetric encryption

25. Buy now–pay now is commonly used for
    (A) Credit cards
    (B) Vaults cards
    (C) Visa cards
    (D) Debit Cards

1.	A B C D	6.	A B C D	11.	A B C D	16.	A B C D	21.	A B C D
2.	A B C D	7.	A B C D	12.	A B C D	17.	A B C D	22.	A B C D
3.	A B C D	8.	A B C D	13.	A B C D	18.	A B C D	23.	A B C D
4.	A B C D	9.	A B C D	14.	A B C D	19.	A B C D	24.	A B C D
5.	A B C D	10.	A B C D	15.	A B C D	20.	A B C D	25.	A B C D

NETWORKING 

LEARNING OBJECTIVES

➤ Basics of computer networking
➤ Types of Topologies
➤ Types of network
➤ Network security

MULTIPLE CHOICE QUESTIONS

1. Which technology has a central device, which brings all the signals together?
   - (A) Bus
   - (B) Star
   - (C) Ring
   - (D) Hybrid

2. Which technology brings a number of computers together, to allow them to share data or resources?
   - (A) Network
   - (B) Interconnection
   - (C) Intercontinental
   - (D) Interuniversity

3. Which cable uses light to transmit data instead of magnetic signals?
   - (A) Coaxial-cables
   - (B) Twisted pair cables
   - (C) Optical fibers
   - (D) Cable optical

4. What are the computers attached to a network called?
   - (A) Nodes
   - (B) Workstations
   - (C) Compu-Machines
   - (D) Both (A) and (B)

5. What is the computer in Networking called?
   - (A) Workstation
   - (B) Server
   - (C) Mainframe
   - (D) None of these

6. The placement of different nodes in a network is called ______.
   - (A) Topology
   - (B) Terminology
   - (C) Placement
   - (D) Layout

7. In which topology all nodes are connected to a common medium along the medium?
   - (A) Bus topology
   - (B) Linear Topology
   - (C) Both (A) and (C)
   - (D) None of these

8. In which Topology, each node is connected to its neighbour on both sides?
   - (A) Ring Topology
   - (B) Bus Topology
   - (C) Mesh Topology
   - (D) Tree Topology

9. Which Topology is the combination of Bus and Star Topology?

(A) Mesh Topology
(B) Fully Connected Topology
(C) Star Topology
(D) Tree Topology

10. PAN Stands for:
(A) Personal Area Network
(B) Personal Area Node
(C) Pacific Area Node
(D) Pacific Area Network

11. Which Network is confined to a local area?
(A) LAN
(B) PAN
(C) WAN
(D) MAN

12. The largest network spread across countries is called:
(A) Arpanet
(B) Intranet
(C) Internet
(D) None of these

13. The cable that connects two or more work-stations are called ________?
(A) Transfer Mode
(B) Connecting star
(C) Transmission Media
(D) Transformer

14. What is the other name of wired media?
(A) WMedia
(B) Guided media
(C) Cabled media
(D) None of these

15. Which of the following is wireless media?
(A) Optical fiber
(B) Satellite
(C) Microwave
(D) Both (B) and (C)

16. Which of the following signals is similar to radio or television signals?
(A) Satellite
(B) Microwave signal
(C) Radiowave signal
(D) Both (A) and (B)

17. MODEM stands for:
(A) Modern Demodern
(B) Mode of Embedding
(C) Modest Demodest
(D) Modulator Demodulator

18. Which device establishes a temporary connection between the source and the destination for communication?
(A) Hub
(B) Switch
(C) Telephone lines
(D) Both (A) and (B)

19. Which device connects dissimilar networks?
(A) Gateway
(B) Bridge
(C) Router
(D) Repeater

20. Which device is used for wireless connection to interconnect mobile phones?
(A) Radiowave
(B) Microwave
(C) Infrared
(D) Bluetooth

21. It is a set of rules and conventions that govern a particular aspect of how devices on a network communicate. TCP/IP, HTTP, POP, FTP are the some examples.
    (A) Protocols
    (B) Software
    (C) Commands
    (D) Both (A) and (B)

22. It describes the layout of the wires and devices as well as the paths used by data transmissions
    (A) Network   (B) Internet
    (C) Protocol   (D) Topology

23. Encryption and decryption are the function of
    (A) Session layer
    (B) Presentation layer
    (C) Transport layer
    (D) None of these

24. What is the use of bridge in network?
    (A) To connect LAN's
    (B) To separate LAN's
    (C) To control network speed
    (D) None of these

25. In OSI network architecture, the routing is performed by
    (A) Data link layer
    (B) Network layer
    (C) Session layer
    (D) Transport layer

Darken Your Choice with HB Pencil

1.	(A) (B) (C) (D)	6.	(A) (B) (C) (D)	11.	(A) (B) (C) (D)	16.	(A) (B) (C) (D)	21.	(A) (B) (C) (D)
2.	(A) (B) (C) (D)	7.	(A) (B) (C) (D)	12.	(A) (B) (C) (D)	17.	(A) (B) (C) (D)	22.	(A) (B) (C) (D)
3.	(A) (B) (C) (D)	8.	(A) (B) (C) (D)	13.	(A) (B) (C) (D)	18.	(A) (B) (C) (D)	23.	(A) (B) (C) (D)
4.	(A) (B) (C) (D)	9.	(A) (B) (C) (D)	14.	(A) (B) (C) (D)	19.	(A) (B) (C) (D)	24.	(A) (B) (C) (D)
5.	(A) (B) (C) (D)	10.	(A) (B) (C) (D)	15.	(A) (B) (C) (D)	20.	(A) (B) (C) (D)	25.	(A) (B) (C) (D)

LATEST DEVELOPMENTS IN 'IT' 

LEARNING OBJECTIVES

➤ Latest developments in the field of IT

MULTIPLE CHOICE QUESTIONS

1. Shared memory is
   (A) A computer architecture where all processors have direct access to common physical memory
   (B) It refers to network based memory access for physical memory that is not common
   (C) A shared memory bus
   (D) None of these

2. Parallel computing can include:
   (A) Single computer with multiple processors
   (B) Arbitrary number of computers connected by a network
   (C) Combination of both a and b
   (D) None of these

3. Latency is:
   (A) Partitioning so that the data associated is decomposed
   (B) Partitioning so that focus is on the computation
   (C) It is the time to send a 0 byte message from point a to point b
   (D) None of these

4. What does UMA stand for
   (A) Uniform memory access
   (B) United management access
   (C) Unconditional memory access
   (D) None of these

5. Data dependence is
   (A) Involves only those tasks executing a communication operation
   (B) It exists between program statements when the order of statement execution affects the results of the program
   (C) It can be considered as minimization of task idle time
   (D) None of these

6. Generally all the browsers are supporting HTML but basically the HTML is used by
   (A) Mosaic browser
   (B) Internet explorer
   (C) Mozilla
   (D) Safari

7. Which of the following statements is/are true?
   (A) WWW is used for accessing any information on the internet

(B) Newsgroups and emails are not part of the web

(C) With the help of hyperlinks the web links one site to another

(D) All of these

8. Which one of the following button is used to display a list of recently visited sites?

(A) Favourites   (B) Home

(C) Refresh   (D) History

9. Which one of the following is not a search engine?

(A) Excite   (B) Snap

(C) Yandex   (D) All of these

10. What does CERN stands for?

(A) Consiel Européen pour la Recherche Nucléaire

(B) Control enumerated ram number

(C) Counsel engine research navigator

(D) None of these

11. Which one of the following is an invalid video resolution?

(A) 640*480

(B) 800*680

(C) 1024*768

(D) 1152*864

12. Which was the first intel processor?

(A) 3080

(B) 4004

(C) 8080

(D) 8086

13. Which of the following is not related to power?

(A) PIO

(B) SURGE

(C) VGA PORT

(D) MODEM

14. ______ is not a DVD drive.

(A) DVD-RD

(B) DVD-RW

(C) DVD+RW

(D) DVD+RAM

15. How many 10 mega pixel photographs can be stored on a 4GB SDcard?

(A) 2770   (B) 1540

(C) 3080   (D) 6160

16. The iphone 5s had a ______.

(A) 2-megapixel camera

(B) 2.7-megapixel camera

(C) 8-megapixel camera

(D) 5-megapixel camera

17. On myspace, what are "moods"?

(A) Myspace fans

(B) E-mail messages

(C) Emoticons

(D) Instant messages

18. A wireless adapter for your PC or laptop plugs into all of the following except:

(A) PS2 port

(B) USB port

(C) PC card slot

(D) None of these

19. What is an Easter Egg?

(A) A secret massage in application typically used to display credits to the development team

(B) A secret message in some software which is displayed on the eve of easter

(C) A dangerous computer virus which was discovered on easter

(D) A mobile operating system released on easter, 2013

20. Which of the following sensors are present in Samsung Galaxy S6?

(A) Magnetometer

(B) Barometer

(C) GyroScope

(D) All of these

21. In which institution have researchers developed and successfully tested an AI tool called "Sybil" that effectively predicts lung cancer risk?
    (A) Stanford University
    (B) Massachusetts Institute of Technology
    (C) Imperial College London
    (D) University of Cambridge

22. The creation of cryptocurrency 'Dogecoin' was inspired by which of these creatures?
    (A) Dog
    (B) Monkey
    (C) Parrot
    (D) Squirrel

23. Which company has unveiled a breakthrough in semiconductor design and process with the development of the world's first chip announced with 2 Nanometer Nanosheet Technology?
    (A) TCS
    (B) Wipro
    (C) IBM
    (D) HCL

24. What is the name of the Worlds 1st Artificial Intelligence Ship?
    (A) Sunflower 40
    (B) Earth 2030
    (C) Mayflower 400
    (D) Seafarer 66

25. The first-ever 3D printed house of India has recently been inaugurated at which place?
    (A) IIT Delhi
    (B) IIT Bengaluru
    (C) IIT Madras
    (D) IIT Kanpur

Darken Your Choice with HB Pencil

1.	A B C D	6.	A B C D	11.	A B C D	16.	A B C D	21.	A B C D
2.	A B C D	7.	A B C D	12.	A B C D	17.	A B C D	22.	A B C D
3.	A B C D	8.	A B C D	13.	A B C D	18.	A B C D	23.	A B C D
4.	A B C D	9.	A B C D	14.	A B C D	19.	A B C D	24.	A B C D
5.	A B C D	10.	A B C D	15.	A B C D	20.	A B C D	25.	A B C D

LOGICAL REASONING

LEARNING OBJECTIVES

- Concept of odd one out
- Different types of series
- Concept of coding and decoding
- Questions of mathematical reasoning
- Mirror images of letters
- Embedded figures basics

MULTIPLE CHOICE QUESTIONS

Directions (1-5): A group of five items is given. Four of them share the common features whereas one of them is different from others. Choose the item which is different from the others.

1. (A) Rupee   (B) Lira
   (C) Coin   (D) Dinar
2. (A) Algebra   (B) Trigonometry
   (C) Geometry   (D) Mathematics
3. (A) Nest   (B) Stable
   (C) Hole   (D) Boat
4. (A) 1 : 1   (B) 2 : 8
   (C) 3 : 27   (D) 5 : 120
5. (A) 17 : 35   (B) 8 : 17
   (C) 15 : 29   (D) 20 : 41

Directions (6–10): Choose the alternative that will complete the series.

6. dfe, jih, mln, ?, vut
   (A) oqp   (B) psr
   (C) prq   (D) rsp
7. ?, ayw, gec, mki, sqo
   (A) zxw   (B) bzw
   (C) usq   (D) may
8. eac, gce, ieg, ?
   (A) Jhi   (B) jgi
   (C) kgi   (D) khi
9. bl, fp, jt, ?, rb, vf
   (A) mw   (B) nx
   (C) oy   (D) mx
10. ?, siy, oeu, kaq, gwm, cri
    (A) wnc   (B) wnb
    (C) vnc   (D) wmc
11. If in a certain language APRIL is coded as BQSJM, then how will MARCH be coded?
    (A) NBSDI   (B) NBQBH
    (C) NBSBG   (D) LZQBI
12. If in a certain language TRAIN is coded as SQZHM, then how will SCOOTER be coded?
    (A) TDPPUFS   (B) RBPPUFS
    (C) RBNNSDS   (D) RBNNSDQ
13. If in a certain language GANGA is coded as ICPIC, then how will YAMUNA be coded?
    (A) ACOWPC   (B) ZBOWPC
    (C) ACOVOB   (D) ACOWPB
14. If in a certain language INCOME is coded as JMDNND, then how will DIRECT be coded?
    (A) EJSFDU   (B) CHQDBS
    (C) EHSDDS   (D) EHSDBS

15. If in a certain language BANK is coded as ZYLI, then how will TAXES be coded?
    (A) RYVCQ   (B) RYBFT
    (C) SZWES   (D) SEXAT

Directions (16–20): If '+' is '×', '–' is '+', '×' is '÷' and '÷' is '–', then answer the following questions based on the given information.

16. $9 \div 5 + 4 - 3 \times 2 = ?$
    (A) 2   (B) –9
    (C) –3   (D) None of these

17. $6 + 7 \times 3 - 8 \div 20 = ?$
    (A) –3   (B) 7
    (C) 2   (D) 1

18. $3 \times 2 + 4 - 2 \div 9 = ?$
    (A) –1   (B) 1
    (C) –2   (D) 3

19. $6 - 9 + 8 \times 3 \div 20 = ?$
    (A) –2   (B) 6
    (C) 10   (D) 12

20. $5 \times 4 - 6 \div 3 + 1 = ?$
    (A) 5   (B) 4
    (C) –1   (D) 2

21. Find the minimum number of straight lines required to make the given figure.

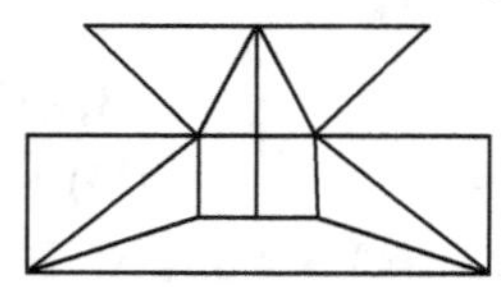

    (A) 16   (B) 17
    (C) 18   (D) 19

22. Find the number of triangles in the given figure.

    (A) 22   (B) 24
    (C) 26   (D) 28

Directions (23–25): On the basis of the information given below, select the correct alternative or answer for the questions that follow:

There are four persons A, B, C and D. One of them is a lecturer and plays football and cricket. A and B are accountants. A plays Badminton. Both the Accountants are Swimmers. D is a bank clerk. One Accountant also plays Tennis. The bank clerk plays carom and is a swimmer. All the four persons play two games each and follow one profession.

23. Who is the lecturer?
    (A) A   (B) D
    (C) C   (D) B

24. Who plays tennis?
    (A) C
    (B) B
    (C) A
    (D) Cannot be determined

25. Who plays tennis and is an accountant?
    (A) D
    (B) B
    (C) A
    (D) C

26. Choose the alternative which most closely resembles the mirror image of the given combination.
    ANS43Q12
    (1) ƧИＡƧＡƐＱＦＳ   (2) ＳＦＱƐＡƧИＡ
    (3) ＳИＡƐＦＱＳＦ   (4) ＦＳＱＡƐＡИＳ
    (A) 1   (B) 2   (C) 3   (D) 4

27. Choose the alternative which most closely resembles the mirror image of the given combination.
    TARA IN1014A
    (1) ＡＦＦＯＦИＩ ＡЯＡꞱ   (2) ＡＦＯＦＦИ Ｉ ＡЯＡＴ
    (3) ＡＦＯＦＦ ＴＡЯＡＩИ   (4) ＡＦＦＯＦИ Ｉ ＡЯＡＴ
    (A) 1   (B) 2   (C) 3   (D) 4

28. Choose the alternative which most closely resembles the mirror image of the given combination.
    1965 INDOPAK
    (1) ꞰＡꟼＯＤИＩ ƧＳ6Ｆ   (2) ꞰＡꟼＯＤИＩ ＦＳ6Ƨ
    (3) ꞰＡꟼＯＤИＩ Ｓ6ＳＦ   (4) ꞰＡꟼＯＤИＩ Ｓ6ＳＦ
    (A) 1   (B) 2   (C) 3   (D) 4

29. Choose the alternative which most closely resembles the mirror image of the given combination.

MALAYALAM

(1) MALAYALAM   (2) MA⅃AYA⅃AM
(3) ⱮA⅃AYA⅃AⱮ   (4) MAᒋAYAᒋAM

(A) 1   (B) 2   (C) 3   (D) 4

30. Choose the alternative which most closely resemble the mirror image of the given combination.

EFFECTIVE

(1) ƎVITƆƎᖷᖷƎ   (2) EVITCEFFE
(3) ƎᖷᖷƆＯTIVƎ   (4) ƎVITƆƎᖷᖷƎ

(A) 1   (B) 2   (C) 3   (D) 4

31. Find out the alternative figure which contains figure (X) as its part.

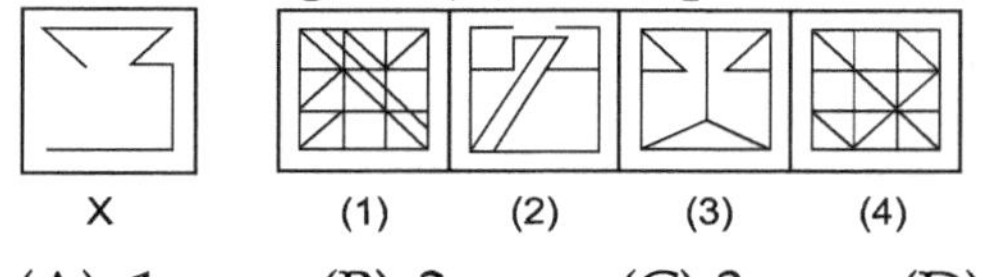

    X   (1)   (2)   (3)   (4)

(A) 1   (B) 2   (C) 3   (D) 4

32. Find out the alternative figure which contains figure (X) as its part.

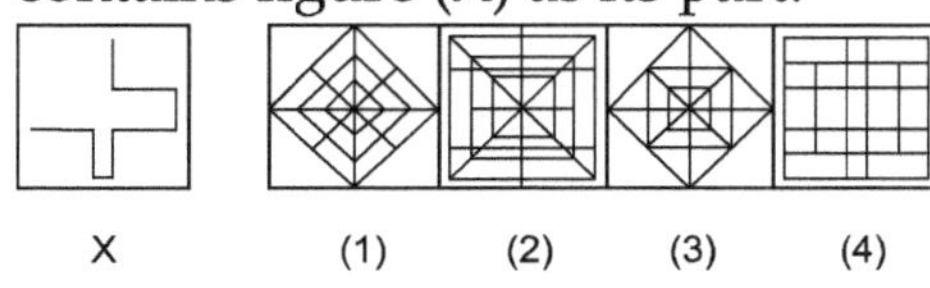

    X   (1)   (2)   (3)   (4)

(A) 1   (B) 2   (C) 3   (D) 4

33. Find out the alternative figure which contains figure (X) as its part.

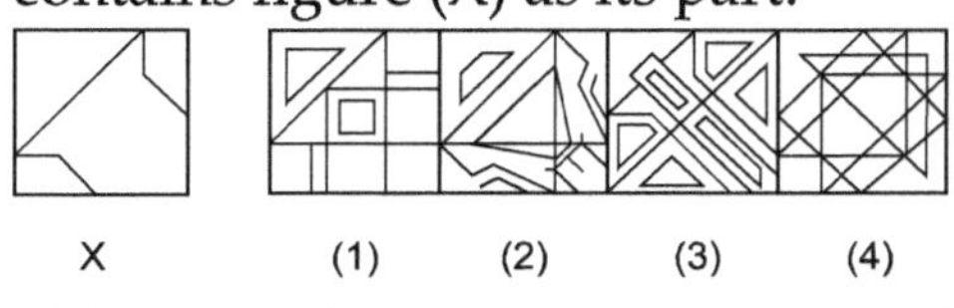

    X   (1)   (2)   (3)   (4)

(A) 1   (B) 2   (C) 3   (D) 4

34. Find out the alternative figure which contains figure (X) as its part.

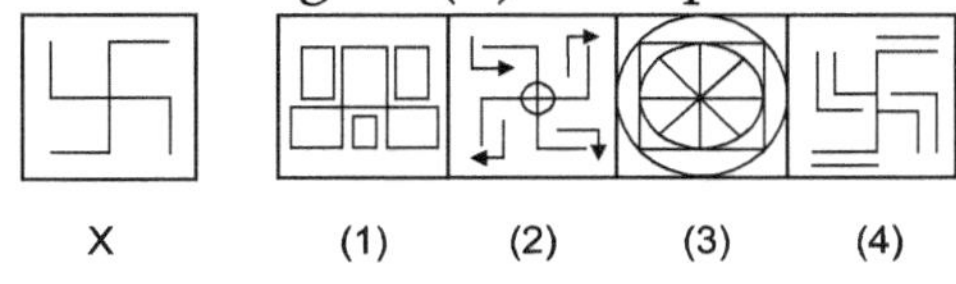

    X   (1)   (2)   (3)   (4)

(A) 1   (B) 2   (C) 3   (D) 4

35. Find out the alternative figure which contains figure (X) as its part.

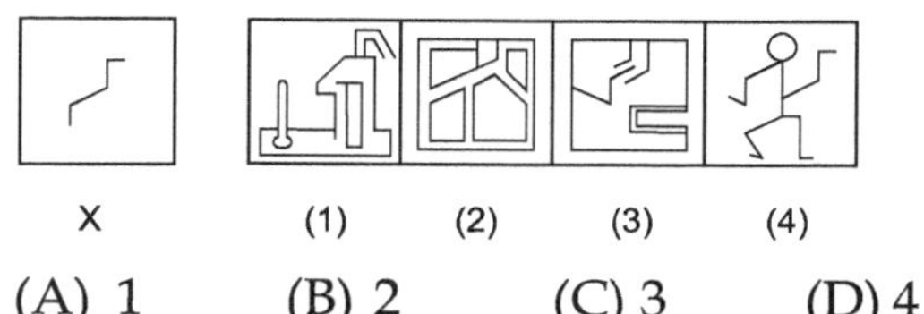

    X   (1)   (2)   (3)   (4)

(A) 1   (B) 2   (C) 3   (D) 4

36. Select a suitable figure from the four alternatives that would complete the figure matrix.

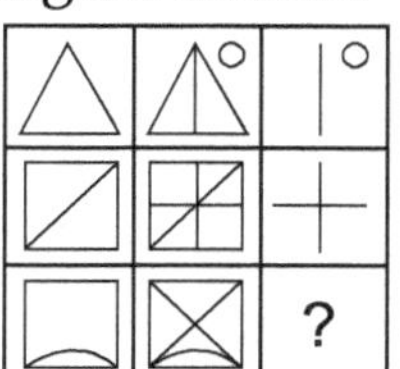

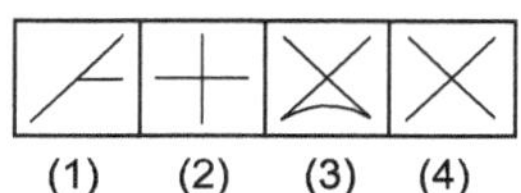

    (1)   (2)   (3)   (4)

(A) 1   (B) 2
(C) 3   (D) 4

37. Select a suitable figure from the four alternatives that would complete the figure matrix.

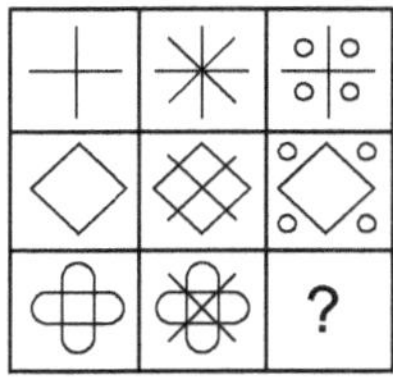

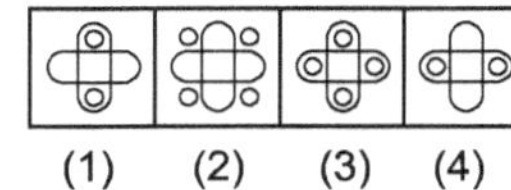

    (1)   (2)   (3)   (4)

(A) 1   (B) 2
(C) 3   (D) 4

38. Select a suitable figure from the four alternatives that would complete the figure matrix.

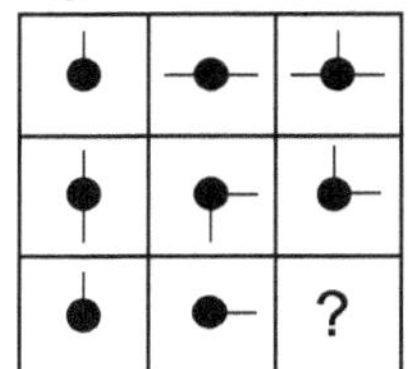

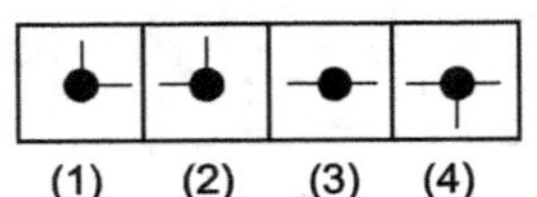

(1)   (2)   (3)   (4)

(A) 1   (B) 2

(C) 3   (D) 4

39. Select a suitable figure from the four alternatives that would complete the figure matrix.

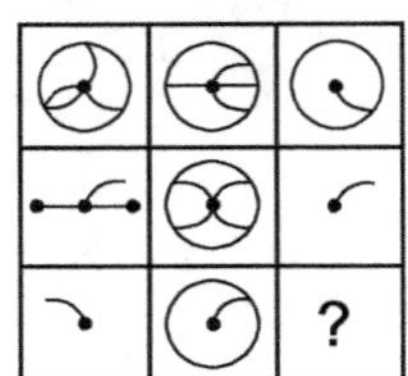

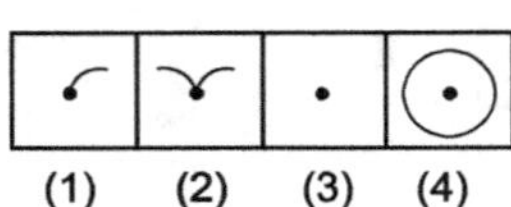

(1)   (2)   (3)   (4)

(A) 1   (B) 2

(C) 3   (D) 4

40. Select a suitable figure from the four alternatives that would complete the figure matrix.

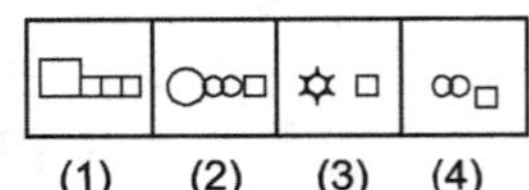

(1)   (2)   (3)   (4)

(A) 1

(B) 2

(C) 3

(D) 4

	A B C D		A B C D		A B C D		A B C D		A B C D
1.	Ⓐ Ⓑ Ⓒ Ⓓ	9.	Ⓐ Ⓑ Ⓒ Ⓓ	17.	Ⓐ Ⓑ Ⓒ Ⓓ	25.	Ⓐ Ⓑ Ⓒ Ⓓ	33.	Ⓐ Ⓑ Ⓒ Ⓓ
2.	Ⓐ Ⓑ Ⓒ Ⓓ	10.	Ⓐ Ⓑ Ⓒ Ⓓ	18.	Ⓐ Ⓑ Ⓒ Ⓓ	26.	Ⓐ Ⓑ Ⓒ Ⓓ	34.	Ⓐ Ⓑ Ⓒ Ⓓ
3.	Ⓐ Ⓑ Ⓒ Ⓓ	11.	Ⓐ Ⓑ Ⓒ Ⓓ	19.	Ⓐ Ⓑ Ⓒ Ⓓ	27.	Ⓐ Ⓑ Ⓒ Ⓓ	35.	Ⓐ Ⓑ Ⓒ Ⓓ
4.	Ⓐ Ⓑ Ⓒ Ⓓ	12.	Ⓐ Ⓑ Ⓒ Ⓓ	20.	Ⓐ Ⓑ Ⓒ Ⓓ	28.	Ⓐ Ⓑ Ⓒ Ⓓ	36.	Ⓐ Ⓑ Ⓒ Ⓓ
5.	Ⓐ Ⓑ Ⓒ Ⓓ	13.	Ⓐ Ⓑ Ⓒ Ⓓ	21.	Ⓐ Ⓑ Ⓒ Ⓓ	29.	Ⓐ Ⓑ Ⓒ Ⓓ	37.	Ⓐ Ⓑ Ⓒ Ⓓ
6.	Ⓐ Ⓑ Ⓒ Ⓓ	14.	Ⓐ Ⓑ Ⓒ Ⓓ	22.	Ⓐ Ⓑ Ⓒ Ⓓ	30.	Ⓐ Ⓑ Ⓒ Ⓓ	38.	Ⓐ Ⓑ Ⓒ Ⓓ
7.	Ⓐ Ⓑ Ⓒ Ⓓ	15.	Ⓐ Ⓑ Ⓒ Ⓓ	23.	Ⓐ Ⓑ Ⓒ Ⓓ	31.	Ⓐ Ⓑ Ⓒ Ⓓ	39.	Ⓐ Ⓑ Ⓒ Ⓓ
8.	Ⓐ Ⓑ Ⓒ Ⓓ	16.	Ⓐ Ⓑ Ⓒ Ⓓ	24.	Ⓐ Ⓑ Ⓒ Ⓓ	32.	Ⓐ Ⓑ Ⓒ Ⓓ	40.	Ⓐ Ⓑ Ⓒ Ⓓ

MULTIPLE CHOICE QUESTIONS

Logical Reasoning

1. Which of these is the odd one out (different from the others)?
   (A) Apple
   (B) Banana
   (C) Potato
   (D) Mango

2. Choose the alternative that will complete the series.
   Y, V, S, P, M, ?
   (A) N
   (B) K
   (C) L
   (D) J

3. If in a certain language TRAIN is coded as SQZHM, then how will SCOOTER be coded?
   (A) TDPPUFS
   (B) RBPPUFS
   (C) RBNNSDS
   (D) RBNNSDQ

4. In a class of 50 students, 18 take music, 26 take art, and 2 take both art and music. How many students in the class are not enrolled in either music or art
   (A) 6
   (B) 8
   (C) 16
   (D) 24

5. What is true about the statement "If two angles are right angles, the angles have equal measure" and its converse "If two angles have equal measure, then the two angles are right angles"?
   (A) The statement is true but its converse is false.
   (B) The statement is false but its converse is true.
   (C) Both the statements and its converse are false.
   (D) Both the statements and its converse are true.

6. If A is the son of Q, Q and Y are sisters, Z is the mother of Y, P is the son of Z, then which of the following statements is correct?
   (A) P is the maternal uncle of A.
   (B) P and Y are sisters.
   (C) A and P are cousins.
   (D) None of these.

7. In the following question, four groups of letters have been given, out of which four are alike in some way and one is different. Choose the odd one out.
   (A) Rule
   (B) Common
   (C) Law
   (D) Custom

8. Choose the correct alternative from the given options to fill in the blank.
   A child should not be as being either very shy or over aggressive.
   (A) Categorized
   (B) Instructed
   (C) Intoned
   (D) Unfocused

9. A swimming pool is being filled with water at a rate of 1 inch/minute. The owners started filling the pool at 6:00 a.m. What time was it when the water got 6 feet deep? (1 feet = 12 inches)
   (A) 6:06 a.m.
   (B) 7:06 a.m.
   (C) 7:00 a.m.
   (D) 7:12 a.m.

10. In a football game, a team lost 13 points on one play, gained 7 on the next and lost 3 on the third. What is their position (gain or loss) from their original position?
    (A) Loss of 3 points
    (B) Loss of 9 points

(C) Gain of 3 points

(D) Gain of 17 points

11. Jill is putting a tile floor in her kitchen. She needs 52 tiles to cover the whole floor. There are 24 tiles in a box. A box costs Rs. 23.95. Individual tiles cost Rs. 2.95. Sales tax is 5%. How much will 52 tiles cost approximately, including sales tax?

(A) Rs. 50   (B) Rs. 57

(C) Rs. 60   (D) Rs. 63

12. Mr. Das Gupta teaches three drama classes. The first class has 24 students. The second class has 30 students. The third class has 18 students. Mr. Das Gupta wants to divide each class into groups so that every group in every class has the same number of students and there are no students left over. What is the maximum number of students that he can put into each group?

(A) 8   (B) 6

(C) 4   (D) 2

13. Which letter will be sixth to the left of the nineteenth letter from the right end of the English alphabet?

(A) M   (B) N

(C) B   (D) Y

14. A painter is given a task to paint a cubical box with six different colours for different faces of the cube. The detailed account of it is given as:

(A) Red face should lie between yellow and brown faces.

(B) Green face should be adjacent to the silver face.

(C) Pink face should lie adjacent to the green face.

(D) Yellow face should lie opposite to the brown one.

(E) Silver and pink faces should lie opposite to each other.

The face opposite to red is ______ .

(A) Yellow   (B) Green

(C) Pink   (D) Silver

15. Four of the following five pairs of alphabets and numerals have same relationship between their elements as in the case of the pair PROBLEM : 2948375 and hence form a group. Which one does not belong to the group?

(A) BORE : 8497   (B) MOEP : 5972

(C) LBOR : 3849   (D) OMEP : 4572

Computers and Information Technology

16. If you press Ctrl + O

(A) The programs opens the file

(B) The programs selects all text

(C) The programs saves the file

(D) The program closes

17. FORTRAN is a

(A) Primary language

(B) Low level language

(C) Medium level language

(D) High level language

18. C++ is a

(A) Primary language

(B) Low level language

(C) Medium level language

(D) High level language

19. MS PowerPoint is used to

(A) Type text

(B) Prepare presentation

(C) Perform calculations

(D) Program a language

20. DVD is a

(A) Primary storing device

(B) Secondary storage device

(C) Volatile memory

(D) Is used to store video and audio files

21. PROM stands for

(A) Programmable Run Only Memory

(B) Programmable Read Only Memory

(C) Programmable Right Only Memory

(D) Programmable Risk Only Memory

22. RAM stands for

(A) Random Access memory

(B) Right Access Memory

(C) Read And Memory
(D) Run Only Memory

23. ALU stands for
(A) Arithmetic Logic Unit
(B) Arithmetical Logical Unit
(C) Arithmetic Loss Unit
(D) Academic Logic Unit

24. MS Excel is used to
(A) Type text
(B) Prepare presentation
(C) Perform calculations
(D) Program a language

25. MicroSoft is owned by
(A) Anil Ambani
(B) Mark Zuckerberg
(C) Bill Gates
(D) Angela Merkel

26. The formula in Excel always starts with a
(A) +
(B) *
(C) =
(D) $

27. Windows Vista is
(A) An operating system
(B) Hardware system
(C) Application software
(D) All of these

28. What happen if you press Ctrl + I in Word?
(A) The text becomes italics
(B) The text gets underlined
(C) The text erases
(D) The text becomes bold

29. Trojan is one of the
(A) Font style
(B) Virus
(C) OS
(D) Output devices

30. iamhappy in iamhappy@yahoo.com is the
(A) Username
(B) Web browser
(C) URL
(C) Domain name

31. The username and the domain name is separated by
(A) %
(B) *
(C) @
(D) !

32. The latest MS Word version in the market is
(A) MS Word 2010
(B) MS Word 2007
(C) MS Word 2008
(D) MS Word 2013

33. MS Access is used to
(A) Used to develop application software
(B) Perform calculations
(C) Prepare presentations
(D) Used to program a language

34. It is one of the network topologies
(A) Wired topology
(B) Mesh topology
(C) Circle topology
(D) Non wired topology

35. A star topology has a central connection point called a
(A) Node
(B) Bud
(C) Hub
(D) Hub node

36. In Flash CS6, which of the following options of the Brush tool is used to paint behind the strokes and the fills in the same layer?
(A) Paint Fills
(B) Paint Selection
(C) Paint Inside
(D) Paint Behind

37. The most popular and the largest WAN connection is the
(A) Intranet
(B) Ethernet
(C) Network
(D) Internet

38. CAN stands for
(A) Car Area Network
(B) Campus Area network
(C) College area network
(D) Combines area network

39. There are ______ types of topology network.
(A) 5
(B) 6
(C) 7
(D) 8

40. It operates at a frequency of 2400 to 2483.5 MHz.
   (A) Watsapp   (B) Bluetooth
   (C) Viber   (D) Webcam

41. The __________ mediates communication between the CPU and the other components of the system, including the main memory.
   (A) ROM   (B) CMOS battery
   (C) Chipset   (D) CPU

42. Outlook is
   (A) Internet browser
   (B) Email service provider
   (C) Antivirus software
   (D) Program software

43. The CMOS battery is same as the
   (A) Mobile battery
   (B) Car battery
   (C) Watch battery
   (D) Torch battery

44. Power supply is measured in
   (A) Voltage   (B) Ampere
   (C) Wattage   (D) Joules

45. The common name for VDU is
   (A) Keyboard   (B) Mouse
   (C) Monitor   (D) Scanner

Achievers Section

46. In MS PowerPoint, you can add
   (A) Animations
   (B) Transition of slides
   (C) Sound
   (D) All of these

47. If you click Shift + Space bar in MS Excel
   (A) The entire row gets selected
   (B) The entire column gets selected
   (C) One cell gets selected
   (D) The entire worksheet gets selected

48. A web browser provides which of the services?
   (A) Close connection
   (B) Receive new page
   (C) Request new page from the source
   (D) Connect to the URL typed by the user

49. Cut Copy and Paste are found in _____ menu
   (A) View   (B) Format
   (C) Edit   (D) Insert

50. Who is the father of computers?
   (A) Pascal   (B) John Napier
   (C) Charles Babbage (D) Newton

—————————————— Darken Your Choice with HB Pencil ——————————————

1.	A B C D	11.	A B C D	21.	A B C D	31.	A B C D	41.	A B C D
2.	A B C D	12.	A B C D	22.	A B C D	32.	A B C D	42.	A B C D
3.	A B C D	13.	A B C D	23.	A B C D	33.	A B C D	43.	A B C D
4.	A B C D	14.	A B C D	24.	A B C D	34.	A B C D	44.	A B C D
5.	A B C D	15.	A B C D	25.	A B C D	35.	A B C D	45.	A B C D
6.	A B C D	16.	A B C D	26.	A B C D	36.	A B C D	46.	A B C D
7.	A B C D	17.	A B C D	27.	A B C D	37.	A B C D	47.	A B C D
8.	A B C D	18.	A B C D	28.	A B C D	38.	A B C D	48.	A B C D
9.	A B C D	19.	A B C D	29.	A B C D	39.	A B C D	49.	A B C D
10.	A B C D	20.	A B C D	30.	A B C D	40.	A B C D	50.	A B C D

HINTS AND SOLUTIONS

1. FUNDAMENTALS OF COMPUTER-HARDWARE AND SOFTWARE

Answer Key

1. (C)	2. (C)	3. (B)	4. (B)	5. (B)	6. (C)	7. (A)	8. (B)	9. (D)	10. (C)
11. (D)	12. (C)	13. (D)	14. (D)	15. (A)	16. (A)	17. (D)	18. (C)	19. (D)	20. (A)

HOTS (ACHIEVERS SECTION)

21. (A)	22. (A)	23. (C)	24. (D)	25. (B)

2. INPUT, OUTPUT, MEMORY AND STORAGE DEVICES

Answer Key

1. (B)	2. (A)	3. (A)	4. (C)	5. (B)	6. (C)	7. (C)	8. (D)	9. (B)	10. (B)
11. (A)	12. (A)	13. (B)	14. (D)	15. (D)	16. (B)	17. (C)	18. (B)	19. (C)	20. (A)

HOTS (ACHIEVERS SECTION)

21. (A)	22. (C)	23. (C)	24. (B)	25. (D)

3. INTRODUCTION TO HTML AND CS6

Answer Key

1. (A)	2. (C)	3. (B)	4. (D)	5. (D)	6. (B)	7. (C)	8. (B)	9. (D)	10. (B)
11. (D)	12. (B)	13. (D)	14. (D)	15. (A)	16. (D)	17. (C)	18. (D)	19. (C)	20. (B)

HOTS (ACHIEVERS SECTION)

21. (C)	22. (A)	23. (D)	24. (D)	25. (A)

4. INTRODUCTION TO FLASH CS6

Answer Key

1. (D)	2. (A)	3. (C)	4. (C)	5. (C)	6. (D)	7. (B)	8. (B)	9. (D)	10. (A)
11. (C)	12. (C)	13. (A)	14. (D)	15. (C)					

HOTS (ACHIEVERS SECTION)

16. (A)	17. (C)	18. (D)	19. (B)	20. (A)

5. MS WORD

Answer Key

1. (C)	2. (A)	3. (D)	4. (A)	5. (C)	6. (B)	7. (C)	8. (D)	9. (B)	10. (B)
11. (C)	12. (C)	13. (C)	14. (A)	15. (C)	16. (B)	17. (B)	18. (A)	19. (B)	20. (B)

HOTS (ACHIEVERS SECTION)

21. (A)	22. (A)	23. (D)	24. (A)	25. (D)

6. MS POWERPOINT

Answer Key

1. (D)	2. (A)	3. (A)	4. (C)	5. (D)	6. (B)	7. (B)	8. (A)	9. (C)	10. (A)
11. (C)	12. (D)	13. (B)	14. (A)	15. (B)	16. (C)	17. (D)	18. (B)	19. (A)	20. (B)

HOTS (ACHIEVERS SECTION)

21. (D)	22. (B)	23. (B)	24. (D)	25. (A)

7. MS EXCEL

Answer Key

1. (C)	2. (A)	3. (C)	4. (C)	5. (C)	6. (D)	7. (B)	8. (C)	9. (A)	10. (D)
11. (C)	12. (C)	13. (D)	14. (B)	15. (D)	16. (B)	17. (B)	18. (D)	19. (D)	20. (D)

HOTS (ACHIEVERS SECTION)

21. (B)	22. (A)	23. (A)	24. (D)	25. (A)

Answer Key

1. (B)	2. (A)	3. (C)	4. (A)	5. (A)	6. (B)	7. (D)	8. (A)	9. (B)	10. (A)
11. (D)	12. (D)	13. (A)	14. (A)	15. (C)	16. (D)	17. (B)	18. (A)	19. (C)	20. (C)

HOTS (ACHIEVERS SECTION)

21. (B)	22. (C)	23. (A)	24. (A)	25. (D)

9. INTERNET AND VIRUSES

Answer Key

1. (D)	2. (B)	3. (C)	4. (C)	5. (C)	6. (C)	7. (B)	8. (B)	9. (C)	10. (B)
11. (C)	12. (C)	13. (D)	14. (A)	15. (D)	16. (D)	17. (D)	18. (A)	19. (C)	20. (B)

HOTS (ACHIEVERS SECTION)

21. (D)	22. (D)	23. (D)	24. (B)	25. (C)

10. NETWORKING

Answer Key

1. (B)	2. (A)	3. (C)	4. (D)	5. (B)	6. (B)	7. (A)	8. (A)	9. (D)	10. (A)
11. (A)	12. (C)	13. (C)	14. (B)	15. (D)	16. (C)	17. (D)	18. (D)	19. (A)	20. (D)

HOTS (ACHIEVERS SECTION)

21. (A)	22. (C)	23. (C)	24. (B)	25. (D)

11. LATEST DEVELOPMENTS IN 'IT'

Answer Key

1. (A)	2. (A)	3. (C)	4. (A)	5. (B)	6. (A)	7. (D)	8. (D)	9. (B)	10. (A)
11. (B)	12. (B)	13. (A)	14. (A)	15. (B)	16. (C)	17. (C)	18. (A)	19. (A)	20. (D)

HOTS (ACHIEVERS SECTION)

21. (B)	22. (A)	23. (C)	24. (C)	25. (C)

Answer Key

1. (C)	2. (D)	3. (D)	4. (D)	5. (C)	6. (D)	7. (C)	8. (C)	9. (B)	10. (D)
11. (A)	12. (D)	13. (A)	14. (C)	15. (A)	16. (D)	17. (C)	18. (A)	19. (C)	20. (D)
21. (B)	22. (D)	23. (C)	24. (B)	25. (B)	26. (B)	27. (D)	28. (D)	29. (B)	30. (A)
31. (A)	32. (D)	33. (D)	34. (C)	35. (D)	36. (D)	37. (B)	38. (A)	39. (C)	40. (A)

1. (C)
Rupee, Lira, Dinar and Dollar stand for the name of the currencies and hence form a group. However, coin is not currency.

2. (D)
All, except mathematics, are its branches.

3. (D)
Stable, Hole, Kennel and Nest are the names given to the living places of horses, insects, fish and birds respectively. However, Boat is means of transportation.

4. (D)
In the five ratios the second number is the cube of the first. However, (d) is the exception.

5. (C)
In the five ratios the second number is one more than the double of the first. However, the ratio 15 : 29 does not follow this rule.

6. (D)
There is a gap of three letters between the first letter of each term and the last letter of each term and the last letter of the next term.

7. (C)
Each term in the series consists of alternate letters in reverse order. The first letter of each term and the last letter of the next term are also alternate.

8. (C)
The first letters of the terms are alternate and similarly the second and the third letters.

9. (B)
Each letter of a term of the series is four steps ahead of the corresponding letter of the preceding term.

10. (D)
The letters in each term are moved four steps backward to obtain the letters of the next term.

11. (A)
Each letter of the given word has moved one step ahead in the code.

12. (D)
Each letter of the given word is replaced a letter, in the alphabetic order in its code with the preceding letter.

13. (A)
Each letter of the given word has moved two steps forward in its alphabetic order to form its code.

14. (C)
Letters placed at odd and even places in the given word respectively move one step forward and backward in the alphabetic order to define the coded word.

15. (A)
Each letter of the given word is moved two steps backward in the alphabetic order to define its code.

21. (B)
The figure may be labelled as shown.

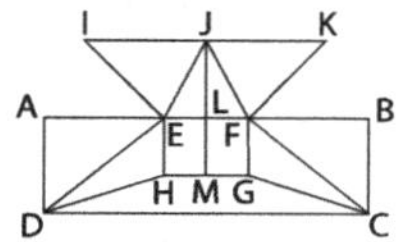

The horizontal lines are IK, AB, HG and DC i.e. 4 in number.

The vertical lines are AD, EH, JM, FG and BC i.e. 5 in number.

The slanting lines are IE, JE, JF, KF, DE, DH, FC and GC i.e. 8 in number.

Thus, there are 4 + 5 + 8 = 17 straight lines in the figure.

22. (D)

The figure may be labelled as shown.

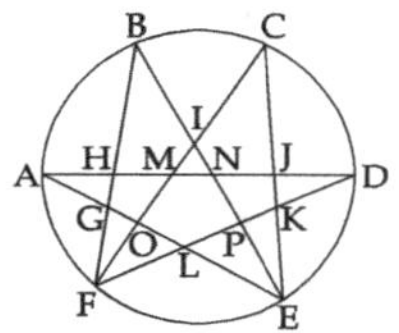

The simplest triangles are AGH, GFO, LFO, DJK, EKP, PEL and IMN i.e. 7 in number.

The triangles having two components each are GFL, KEL, AMO, NDP, BHN, CMJ, NEJ and HFM i.e. 8 in number.

The triangles having three components each are IOE, IFP, BIF and CEI i.e. 4 in number.

The triangles having four components each are ANE and DMF i.e. 2 in number.

The triangles having five components each are FCK, BGE and ADL i.e. 3 in number.

The triangles having six components each are BPF, COE, DHF and AJE i.e. 4 in number.

Total number of triangles in the figure
= 7 + 8 + 4 + 2 + 3 + 4 + 28

(23–25)

The data given in the question can be summarized in the table as under:

Sports Persons	Lect.	Acc	Clerk	Football	Swim	Carom	Bad.	Tenn	Crick
A		*			*		*		
B		*			*			*	
C	*			*					*
D			*		*	*			

31. (A)

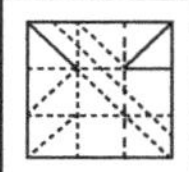

32. (D)

33. (D)

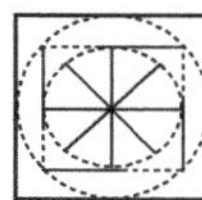

34. (C)

35. (D)

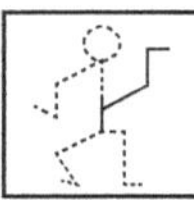

MODEL TEST PAPER

Answer Key

1. (C)	2. (D)	3. (D)	4. (B)	5. (A)	6. (A)	7. (B)	8. (A)	9. (D)	10. (B)
11. (D)	12. (B)	13. (C)	14. (B)	15. (B)	16. (A)	17. (D)	18. (C)	19. (B)	20. (B)
21. (B)	22. (A)	23. (A)	24. (C)	25. (C)	26. (C)	27. (A)	28. (A)	29. (B)	30. (A)
31. (C)	32. (D)	33. (A)	34. (B)	35. (C)	36. (D)	37. (D)	38. (B)	39. (D)	40. (B)
41. (C)	42. (B)	43. (C)	44. (C)	45. (C)	46. (D)	47. (A)	48. (D)	49. (C)	50. (C)

SAMPLE OMR ANSWER SHEET

1. STUDENT NAME (IN ENGLISH CAPITAL LETTERS ONLY)

Students must write and darken the respective circles completely using HB Pencil only. Othewise their Answer Sheets will not be evaluated.

PERSONAL DETAILS

2. SCHOOL CODE

3. CLASS

4. SECTION

5. ROLL NO.

6. QUESTION PAPER SET

A ○
B ○
C ○
D ○

7. MOBILE NUMBER

8. GENDER

MALE ○
FEMALE ○

9. STREAM
(Only for Class XI and XII Students)

MATHEMATICS ○
BIOLOGY ○
OTHERS ○

MARK YOUR ANSWERS

No.	A	B	C	D	No.	A	B	C	D
1.	Ⓐ	Ⓑ	Ⓒ	Ⓓ	26.	Ⓐ	Ⓑ	Ⓒ	Ⓓ
2.	Ⓐ	Ⓑ	Ⓒ	Ⓓ	27.	Ⓐ	Ⓑ	Ⓒ	Ⓓ
3.	Ⓐ	Ⓑ	Ⓒ	Ⓓ	28.	Ⓐ	Ⓑ	Ⓒ	Ⓓ
4.	Ⓐ	Ⓑ	Ⓒ	Ⓓ	29.	Ⓐ	Ⓑ	Ⓒ	Ⓓ
5.	Ⓐ	Ⓑ	Ⓒ	Ⓓ	30.	Ⓐ	Ⓑ	Ⓒ	Ⓓ
6.	Ⓐ	Ⓑ	Ⓒ	Ⓓ	31.	Ⓐ	Ⓑ	Ⓒ	Ⓓ
7.	Ⓐ	Ⓑ	Ⓒ	Ⓓ	32.	Ⓐ	Ⓑ	Ⓒ	Ⓓ
8.	Ⓐ	Ⓑ	Ⓒ	Ⓓ	33.	Ⓐ	Ⓑ	Ⓒ	Ⓓ
9.	Ⓐ	Ⓑ	Ⓒ	Ⓓ	34.	Ⓐ	Ⓑ	Ⓒ	Ⓓ
10.	Ⓐ	Ⓑ	Ⓒ	Ⓓ	35.	Ⓐ	Ⓑ	Ⓒ	Ⓓ
11.	Ⓐ	Ⓑ	Ⓒ	Ⓓ	36.	Ⓐ	Ⓑ	Ⓒ	Ⓓ
12.	Ⓐ	Ⓑ	Ⓒ	Ⓓ	37.	Ⓐ	Ⓑ	Ⓒ	Ⓓ
13.	Ⓐ	Ⓑ	Ⓒ	Ⓓ	38.	Ⓐ	Ⓑ	Ⓒ	Ⓓ
14.	Ⓐ	Ⓑ	Ⓒ	Ⓓ	39.	Ⓐ	Ⓑ	Ⓒ	Ⓓ
15.	Ⓐ	Ⓑ	Ⓒ	Ⓓ	40.	Ⓐ	Ⓑ	Ⓒ	Ⓓ
16.	Ⓐ	Ⓑ	Ⓒ	Ⓓ	41.	Ⓐ	Ⓑ	Ⓒ	Ⓓ
17.	Ⓐ	Ⓑ	Ⓒ	Ⓓ	42.	Ⓐ	Ⓑ	Ⓒ	Ⓓ
18.	Ⓐ	Ⓑ	Ⓒ	Ⓓ	43.	Ⓐ	Ⓑ	Ⓒ	Ⓓ
19.	Ⓐ	Ⓑ	Ⓒ	Ⓓ	44.	Ⓐ	Ⓑ	Ⓒ	Ⓓ
20.	Ⓐ	Ⓑ	Ⓒ	Ⓓ	45.	Ⓐ	Ⓑ	Ⓒ	Ⓓ
21.	Ⓐ	Ⓑ	Ⓒ	Ⓓ	46.	Ⓐ	Ⓑ	Ⓒ	Ⓓ
22.	Ⓐ	Ⓑ	Ⓒ	Ⓓ	47.	Ⓐ	Ⓑ	Ⓒ	Ⓓ
23.	Ⓐ	Ⓑ	Ⓒ	Ⓓ	48.	Ⓐ	Ⓑ	Ⓒ	Ⓓ
24.	Ⓐ	Ⓑ	Ⓒ	Ⓓ	49.	Ⓐ	Ⓑ	Ⓒ	Ⓓ
25.	Ⓐ	Ⓑ	Ⓒ	Ⓓ	50.	Ⓐ	Ⓑ	Ⓒ	Ⓓ

Signature of the Student & Date of Examination

Signature of the Invigilator & Date of Examination